The Night

ЅƎƆⱯꟼ ⱯИIƆⱯꟻ | FACING PAGES

Nicholas Jenkins
Series Editor

AFTER EVERY WAR
Twentieth-Century Women Poets
translations from the German by Eavan Boland

HORACE, THE ODES
New Translations by Contemporary Poets
edited by J. D. McClatchy

HOTHOUSES
Poems 1889, by Maurice Maeterlinck
translated by Richard Howard

LANDSCAPE WITH ROWERS
Poetry from the Netherlands
translated and introduced by J. M. Coetzee

THE NIGHT
by Jaime Saenz
translated and introduced by Forrest Gander and Kent Johnson

The Night

Jaime Saenz

Translated and Introduced by
Forrest Gander and Kent Johnson

With an Afterword by Luis H. Antezana

Princeton University Press
Princeton and Oxford

    Library of Congress Cataloging-in-Publication Data
    Saenz, Jaime.
    [Noche. English]
    The night / Jaime Saenz ; translated by Forrest Gander and Kent Johnson.
    p.   cm. — (Facing pages)
    Includes bibliographical references.
    ISBN-13: 978-0-691-12483-4 (cl. : alk. paper)
    ISBN-10: 0-691-12483-3 (cl. : alk. paper)
    I. Gander, Forrest, 1956–   II. Johnson, Kent.   III. Title.   IV. Series.
    PQ7819.S22N6313   2007
    861'.64—dc22   2006043896

    British Library Cataloging-in-Publication Data is available
    This book has been composed in Janson
    Printed on acid-free paper. ∞
    pup.princeton.edu
    Printed in the United States of America

    10 9 8 7 6 5 4 3 2 1

Contents

Acknowledgments

The translators are grateful for a grant from the PEN Translation Fund, a fellowship in translation from the National Endowment for the Arts, and a Salomon Award from Brown University.

They would like to thank their terrific editors at Princeton University Press, Hanne Winarsky and Nicholas Jenkins, for their close readings, helpful suggestions, and steady enthusiasm.

Gracias also to Alicia Ridenour for her invaluable assistance and to Linda Norton for her early encouragements.

Thanks to Ayelet Ammitay whose translation of the Afterword, later modified by Johnson and Gander, was enormously helpful.

Sections of this poem have been published in the following journals, whose editors the translators would like to especially thank: *Mandorla 7*; *The New Review of Literature*, Fall 2004; *No: A Journal of the Arts*, Spring 2004; *TriQuarterly 119*; *Jacket* (online), August 2004; *Octopus* (online), June 2004.

Photo credits: Chola paceña by Forrest Gander; condor by Steve Metz (stevemetzphotography.com); other photos used with permission of Saenz estate and Luis Antezana.

The Night

Introduction

Notes from Bolivia

Some Things You Should Know about Jaime Saenz

It was with a human leg pilfered from the medical lab that Jaime Saenz, Bolivia's visionary and most influential poet, came home from the university one evening. He was in his mid-forties, still living with his mother, teaching an occasional class on poetry, but obsessed full-time with death, his most constant companion.

In his strange, late poems, visualizing the body as an abode of unfathomable space, as an otherness we carry with us, one that will come to carry us away into itself, Saenz meditated on death. Channeling its plutonic voice, he would come to write, "I am the body who inhabits you, and I am here in the darkness, and I suffer you, and live you, and die you. / But I am not your body. I am the night."

Before writing those lines, though, the young poet first had to bear, through one singular night, for who knows what manner of study, the limb of a cadaver. And in the morning, he punctually presented himself at his clerk's job with the United States Information Service at the U.S. Embassy.

Figure 1. Saenz with U.S. Embassy personnel, ca. mid-1960s, mysteriously rubbing his hands before an early-version computer. In his late poetry, Saenz will excoriate the technology of war and condemn the technophiles to the ninth circle of Hell

Eventually, of course, the police were summoned. You can't keep a human leg hidden under your bed while you live with your mother.

Still, on weekends afterwards, the poet found occasion to visit the morgue.

His book *Recorrer esta distancia* (*To Cross This Distance*) opens with the speaker gazing upon a cadaver. As the poem progresses, we begin to realize that this speaker is a literally disembodied voice meditating upon its own lost body across the distance of the reader's mind.

For Saenz, poetry is the practice of seeing through another consciousness from the afterlife. In the body of a poem, life and death, self and other are enfolded. The final movement of *To Cross This Distance* is spoken—the whole poem leads up to this—from inside the reader, and with such immanent tenderness that the matter of who touches or is touched, kisses, or is kissed, dissipates in the mystery of fused, shared being.

So Jaime Saenz, throughout his life, "experimented" with death. He was hospitalized three times. He insisted to his friends that when he died, they were to cut his carotid arteries. That promise was kept. Saenz was terrified of waking up in a coffin.

When he writes about death and life giving birth to each other, enchanting each other, expanding the realm of ordinary experience, he isn't being rhetorical or merely reveling in paradox. He is articulating a philosophy.

Or a teleology. In Cochabamba, Luis Antezana, an illustrious literary critic and a close friend of the poet, tells us that Jaime Saenz had chosen the more difficult life of a mystic, the *via negativa*. Saenz, Antezana said, was looking for a Gnostic vision. He found god in drugs, alcohol, the street, the body, and death. In a way, he was like the medieval flagellates who drove their bodies into delirium and ruin. Saenz felt that since god had not come to him, he would cross this distance himself. He had his sense of humor to protect him as the distance closed.

Humor: there is plenty to go around at a drinking party of Bolivian literati. After we present our first book of translations of Jaime Saenz's poetry (*Immanent Visitor: Selected Poems of Jaime Saenz*) to a full house at CEDOAL, Bolivia's principal cultural center, people gather at a bar in Sopocachi, a fashionable section of town. When we both stand, somewhat ceremoniously, to make a toast to Saenz, one of Bolivia's prominent critics jumps up, clacks his heels, and extends his arm in mock Fascist salute. No one seems discomfited by the gesture except us.

I lean over and ask a fairly inebriated Humberto Quino, one of Bolivia's big-name poets, what he thinks about Saenz's early Nazi sympathies. "Oh, no, no, it's no big thing, you know, and nothing very surprising," he says. "Saenz was a great poet in the tradition of San Juan and Sor Juana de la Cruz, fascinated by death and the occult, and in his youth he was very seduced by mystical fascist ideology, you see. In politics, he is a bit like Pound, Celine, Heidegger, Mishima, even Pessoa and Borges, eh. . . . You know Borges spoke fawningly of the dictator Videla, and praised his 'iron hand' during the 'Dirty War,' no? Well, except these guys professed their fascism when they were all grown up! Saenz was a kid strutting around Wiesbaden in high boots. But who gives a damn? Long live poetry!"[1] I mention to him that political allegiance is not considered irrelevant in the United States. "Yes, yes, sure," he says, "but isn't it fantastic that the little fascist came to be such a big and freaky poet? Look, there's a big movement of young, working-class poets and artists in Bolivia right now. They live up there on the hills of El Alto in concrete-block houses with no plumbing. Almost all of them are of the hard left. They want to burn down Kentucky Fried Chicken and send the bourgeoisie to the salt flats of Uyuni to be eaten by flamingoes. Who is their number one poetic hero? Saenz! Isn't that beautiful? Long live poetry!"

[1] It is important to note that Borges was actually a political conservative who was also an ardent anti-fascist, and he stood against the rise of fascism in the 1930s when significant numbers of Latin American writers and artists enthusiastically supported its European manifestations—including some who later became prominently identified with Marxism. While Borges did indeed offer lamentable endorsements of the vicious far-right Chilean and Argentine juntas late in his life, some of which he later repudiated, it bears emphasizing that he publicly attacked fascism throughout its officially sanctioned apogee in the Peronist era. And he courageously stood up against anti-Semitism as early as 1934, in his essay "I, a Jew." We thank Eliot Weinberger for pointing out the need for this clarification.

On his wedding night, Jaime Saenz bought and brought home a panther.

It slept with the newlyweds until it grew too large and his wife finally said that it was either her or the panther.

La Paz, That Thin-Aired and Scarcely Believable City

Without foreknowledge, we arrive in La Paz on the day of the solstice, the Aymara new year.[2] The streets are bright with the breathy, joyous crossing melodies of pipes and Andean flutes. Unlike most other Latin American capitals, La Paz is an overwhelmingly indigenous city. Most of the women along the street are Aymara, *cholas paceñas* in elaborate heavy skirts, called polleras, and derby hats, their rainbow-colored *rebozos* (portage or carrying shawls) full as spinnakers over their backs.

What fills the spinnakers blows toward the past. And yet the women on the street tread forward, hunched, their domed bowlers like dark beacons. Invisible, the *aparapitas*[3] in their stitched, bricolaged rai-

---

[2] The Aymara are a large Andean indigenous group living in the vast windy Titicaca plateau of the central Andes in modern Peru, Bolivia, and Chile, numbering up to two million.

[3] As Luis Antezana explains in his afterword to our translation of *The Night*: "One of Saenz's most famous characters is the *aparapita* of La Paz. An aparapita is an indigenous immigrant—more precisely, an Andean Indian or 'Aymara'—who lives in poverty in the city and its fringe neighborhoods. Although one can imagine him as an actual homeless man of the large Western cities, an aparapita is not a drifter or a beggar; mostly, he works as a porter in the public markets or in the transportation centers and stockyards. In Saenz's world, the aparapitas also frequent the garbage dumps and spend their nights drinking alcohol in taverns. When he knows his life has run its course, an aparapita works tirelessly to make enough money to drink himself to death. When he finally dies, his few belongings are inherited by his fellow aparapitas and his anonymous body ends up in the morgue. Nevertheless, according to local beliefs, his 'spirit' now protects his friends in the tavern."

Figure 2. Saenz seated in his writing room, map of La Paz behind him

ment, drink to the dregs, barely speaking, sunk in dank, unmarked bodegas, knowing, as Saenz affirmed, that they know nothing and know everything, everything that matters in the end. The man with a briefcase smartly clicks his little cell phone shut and squats, unsmiling, to have his future read in cards by a brujo.

The city clings to a landscape that resembles a grooved funnel. A mountain-rimmed vortex of congested streets eases us down to

Figure 3. Chola paceña on the streets of La Paz

Plaza San Francisco and the central street that drains away into the wealthier neighborhoods of La Paz.

Pigeons and vendors and everyone waiting for anyone loiter in Plaza San Francisco beside a church notable for its baroque-mestizo architecture. Even in June, Bolivia's winter, the sun is intense. A businessman holds his newspaper to the side of his head while he talks to a pineapple vendor. Hawkers hold forth fake fossil trilobites. The *voceadores*—those who shout the litany of stops from passing minibuses—can be heard here as on every street in La Paz. And scores of bootblacks ply the crowd. The younger ones wear ski masks, despite the heat, in order to keep from being recognized by family or friends.

One approaches us. His boot brush blurs. The drying foam of his spit flecks the wool hole around his mouth. I smile and give him a tip, and he winks and says in a seductive voice, "Nos veremos, Señor Afortunado" (We'll be seeing one another, Fortuned Sir).

On the cathedral's facade, Inca gods and snakes and fruit mix it up with the Apostles. And in each of the thousands of stone blocks there are fading Greek letters, carved there by indigenous masons, almost four hundred years back. It's a mystery, those letters. Some think there may be a code written into the cathedral—cut and scrambled by the toilers. Inside, the church is vast and dark; garish, peeling saints glare sternly down at the supplicants, or peer erotically heavenward, stigmatic and aureoled, bolted to the walls from their backs with massive mahogany screws.

In the cathedral square, an old man indicates to me with one of his stumps to put the coins in his coat pocket.

Those who dare to cross the class 5 rapids of Avenida Prado put their lives at stake.

A woman is singing, "Sopa de cerdo, un peso, un peso."

Across town, hundreds of men and women are marching and chanting slogans for workers' rights. A taxi driver explains to us the merits of nationalizing the petroleum industry. In a bar near the university, artists and writers drink and joke in groups or read alone at a table with an orange juice. On our first day in La Paz, we are told that a llama fetus is buried under every house and every municipal building in the city. For luck. We return to our own neighborhood and an alley full of *hechiceros* (shamans) who promise to read the future in patterns of coca leaves they scatter over a blanket.

Imaginary and Real Photographs

Now a respected poet in his own right, one of Jaime Saenz's pro-
tégés describes him seated on the curb with an old man by Plaza San
Francisco. Saenz spoke little Aymara. The other man spoke little
Spanish. They were passing a bottle back and forth.

On the Aymara new year, the day we arrive, the hechiceros on
Avenida Linares take big swigs of clear alcohol and then spit it back
onto the fire, yelling a blessing, the fire fueled by rags, herbs, fruit,
llama fetuses, palm votives of Pachamama. When the men spit, the
flames spurt up, speaking back. The bottle is passed from hand to
hand. The fire grows and smells acrid, weird. Men in suits hold the
hands of hechiceros and kiss them on the cheek. People arrive, bear-
ing the clear alcohol as a gift. In this crowd of celebrants we are the
strangers, looking in. The bottle is never offered us. No one looks at
us nor speaks to us. We are simply not there.

Late at night, at the house of Jaime's younger sister, we are shown
many photographs. One of them is of his only child, the girl born
of his German Jewish wife, who was an organizer for the Bolivian
fascists just before World War II. Jaime Saenz never saw his
daughter at the age she is in this photograph, about sixteen, with
long dark hair and dramatic, sad, mascaraed eyes. After the war,
when the child was still a baby, her unhappy mother, giving up on
the marriage (and, one presumes, the politics), hauled her back to
Germany.

Only with Saenz could something like this be real: a Jewish Nazi
spouse, with an Amazonian panther on their conjugal bed. So, yes,
let's talk about it: It is the most discomfiting fact that Saenz was a
member of the Bolivian Nazi Youth in his late teens. And it is most

Figure 4. Portrait of the artist as a young Hitler Youth recruit

discomfiting he never went on record as regretting it. In love with the idea of the German—an idea of considerable historical weight in Bolivia—he joined when he was around sixteen and sailed to Germany, with his twenty-five-member scholarship brigade, in September, 1938. He remained until late 1939, working on construction projects and undergoing rigorous military training.

Saenz claimed with bravado to have fought against Titoist forces in Yugoslavia, but this has been disproved by facts of chronology. One would like to be able to say that he unambiguously renounced his political past. But it is simply not clear what his attitude toward fascism became later in life. He remained an avid reader of Heidegger, Nietzsche, and German Romanticism until his death. Like Pound, he elected to distance himself via silence from the matter of his earlier affiliations. Whatever the case, this much can be said: There is no evident mark of anti-Semitism or racism in his voluminous work (poetry, fiction, criticism, drama, and nonfiction); to the contrary, a profound and prolific empathy for the oppressed—the non-Spanish, the laborers, the homosexuals, the outcasts—is to be found there. And in the great indigenous and working class revolution of 1952 against the right-wing oligarchy that had long ruled his nation, Saenz put his military training from Germany to use, fighting on the barricades with miners, shopkeepers, students, and Aymara. Juan Lechin, Latin America's leading Trotskyist, and the country's most influential Marxist thinker, became a close friend and correspondent. And in *The Night*, Saenz paints the plotters of the attempted fascist coup of October, 1979 (led by the infamous General Natush Busch) as flesh-eating demons. How to explain this aparapita's coat of ideological paradoxes? Can it be explained? In what way, exactly— with this poet whose very grammar is Janus-faced with paradox— should it be?

A photograph records a meeting of Saenz with two acolytes of the Krupp Workshops, the notorious, highly influential group who gathered around Jaime Saenz. A brilliant, outsider poet, Saenz would advertise the Krupp Workshops by posting fliers that described a variety of bizarre literary exercises the attendants might expect to attempt. The first page of one of those announcements reads that the "Convocation" has been beamed by means of telepathy to all the "subsidiary" *cacho* (the Andean version of "craps") branches of the world. Under "Retadores" (Challengers) are the compulsory pseudonyms to be adopted by the players elected from the many applicants. Saenz was always game master, the "Jurjizada." It was a kind of Jack Spicer Magic Workshop, but more demanding.

On Miraflores Avenue, there are four different houses in which Saenz lived. As each lease expired, with rent payments due, he

Figure 5. Meeting of the Krupp Workshop

moved farther away from the city into the quiet, which he loved, but also into isolation.

The opening of *The Night* records that aloneness in the last house in which he lived, La Casa del Poeta, and the terrors that often entered it:

> The night, its feelers twitching in the distance
>
> the night locked into a box swallowed by the night in the desk in the nook
>
> while my eyes and especially that space between my eyes and nostrils stretches the length of a two-story gutter
>
> startled and unnerved, I'm suddenly aware—there's a tubular cocoon, spun between my eyes, through which I see only the night, fractured and phantasmagoric

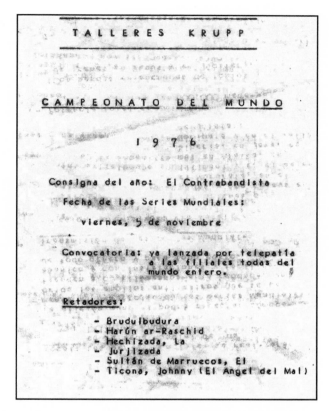

Figure 6. Announcement of Krupp Workshops. Reproduced from Blanca Wiethüchter's *Memoria Solicitada*, a narrative centered on her apprenticeship to, and deep friendship with, Saenz

thanks to a force from who knows where the space of my dream has been split by a wall

on this side sleep is not possible and on the other it's perfectly possible but nevertheless thoroughly impossible

the wall, in fact, is not a wall but a live thing that writhes and throbs and this wall is me

Figure 7. Saenz dreams below a portrait of him by Enrique Arnal

He rarely left his room in his last years. To see him, it was necessary to take a taxi to his house. He might be found lying in bed, drinking a cup of maté with seven sugars and reading a new poem to his friend, the young poet Blanca Wiethüchter. It is her dissertation for the Sorbonne on his body of work that will first bring him major critical attention.

The memorable evening at Blanca's art- and antique-filled house with her husband Alberto Villalpando, and their daughters and their companions: Blanca brings out Saenzian treasures bequeathed to her—photos, letters, the original typescripts of *The Cold, Death by Feel, To Cross This Distance*, all with many notations in his hand. And there is an unpublished libretto for an opera scored by Alberto, Bolivia's most famous composer. The opera is never produced because Saenz decides at the last minute that he will not allow it. He apparently never explains why. "All he said on the phone," says Alberto, "is 'No, it's impossible, it can't be done.' So I said, 'What the hell do

you mean, Jaime? We've spent more than two years on this thing!'
And he just says, 'No, no, it's impossible, it can't be done.' And that
was the last time we ever directly spoke."

El Montículo is a park at the precipice of a hill in the Sopocachi
zone that Saenz loved to visit. At the upper end of a cobblestone
street, it is a lover's park with baroque colonnades and the stanzas of
a tango to Mount Illimani inscribed on four rocks along the en-
trance path. From El Montículo it is possible to see the distant,
upper limits of the city, where streets abrupt into sheer cliff faces
which, when it rains, crumble into the lower precincts of the neigh-
borhood appropriately called Tembladerani. Along those cliffs,
Saenz and his friend Leonardo Garcia Pabón used to hike toward
the massive vertical limestone rise called Llojata. Here, they could
take one step forward, behind Llojata, and enter a sepulchral si-
lence. Or they could take one step backwards and hear again the
clamor of the city echoing up the mountain.

At a party at the poet Humberto Quino's house, nestled beneath the
stalagmite-like towers of Llojata, we meet the editors of Bolivia's
leading literary journal, *Global Lepidoptera*. They publish the great
Latin American poets unknown to us. And they've translated Dick-
inson, Whitman, Pound, Eliot, Williams, Auden, Lowell, Plath, and
Ginsberg, among others. News of our more recent poetry hasn't
reached them yet—just as almost none of Bolivia's more recent po-
etry has reached us. In fact, almost none of their literature has
reached us, modernist or postmodern.

Perhaps it was from El Montículo that Saenz began to form his
idea—seriously held, from all accounts—that La Paz was cupped on
a thin shell of rock over a vast chasm, and that one day the shell
would break and the city fall, like a yolk, into the fathomless Hades
beneath it.

First Day in La Paz

Overheard conversation: Don't let the taxi driver turn the lights out at night. Ask him to turn them back on.

There is a passage in the third section of *The Night* where Saenz, in drunk elation, gives the *taxista* his multivolume *Complete Works of Nietzsche* as payment for the fare, and the man drives away, never to be seen again.

Although men are the same, urinals are curiously different from country to country. These are petaled like orchids and fairly low to the floor.

Singani and Pico de Macho at El Rey, surrounded by mirrors on green stucco. The Pico de Macho, a hot dish of shredded pork, makes us take gulps of water with every bite. The singani, a traditional drink, a mix of hard liquor and wine, tastes something of a cross between apple juice and codeine. Returning to our hotel in taxi, we come across large, happy crowds lining El Prado, as if waiting for a parade. The taxi driver tells us that they are indeed waiting for some kind of big parade, a *desfile*, but he isn't sure what kind. The next morning we open the paper and read that La Paz has experienced its very first march for gay rights, and the photos show that it has been a most festive event, by all accounts a great success, with nary an instance of harassment. The reporting, on TV and in the papers, is quite supportive of the march, which, we read, was headed by a purposeful contingent of indigenous lesbians in bowler hats and polleras. It was Jaime Saenz who wrote *Los Papeles de Narciso Lima-Acha*, the first novel in Bolivia— and one of the very first in Latin America—to openly deal with homosexual themes.

A man with a mustache and a blind, milky eye approaches our table to tell us that we look like strangers, and the beer we are drinking, Paceña, is vastly inferior to the other local beer, Huari.

Later that day, at a bar some streets away, a tall man with dark, slicked-back hair and Errol Flynn mustache sits down at the table next to ours. He engages us, and we come to find out he used to be a captain in the Bolivian Armed Forces, dishonorably discharged through a "framing," he claims, an event that has led to his losing everything, including his family. Still, he wears an impeccably pressed suit and looks quite dashing. He is writing a novel, "a historical one, like *War and Peace*," and we discover that its plot is informed by an exaltation of all things Spanish, and a debasement of most things indigenous, for, he tells us, it is Indian culture that has been the ball and chain of the nation, kept it mired in superstition and despair. Having noticed that he appears to be packing an object beneath his coat, we choose to change the subject rather than to challenge, and come to hear much about the government's and military's complicity in the cocaine trade, for in the army he "saw things that are hard to believe." And we learn from him that the U.S. is perfectly aware of the Bolivian military's involvement in the coke trade and for all intents and purposes turns a blind eye. "It's a dark and dangerous world," he pronounces, smoke issuing from his nose. "And it's not for sissies." Then he begins to talk about the Indians again, and of all their maladies, and we make up an excuse to leave. Outside, we both agree he reminded us of the figure in "The Gatekeeper" section of *The Night*, the tall, mustachioed man with gummed hair parted down the middle, who approaches the delirious Saenz in his bed, gleefully rubbing his hands and making little bows, who tickles him under the arms, head-butts him in the chest, and then plunges a butcher knife into his groin.

Ignoring us completely, two men in black leather coats and three in white shirts with alpaca jackets, sitting as close as lovers around one small table, throw the dice relentlessly.

As Saenz did with his acolytes in the *Kreis*-like[4] meetings of Los Talleres Krupp, Saenz as Stefan George, of course, and the main game was called *cacho* (craps). We hear stories of Saenz flying into a rage when he lost: rage not at having been beaten in a game of talent or wits (apparently he was a perfectly good loser at chess and checkers), but in a game of pure chance, as if the gods were arrayed against him in the dice.

Someone mutters *"yanqui"* as I pass and after a few more steps I pause, thinking I might respond in some thoughtful way to rehabilitate his estimation of me, but when I look back, I see he has been studying me the whole time and he waves his hands dismissively and crosses the street.

We eat tongue and *tunta*, an ancient potato that can be stored for thirty years, we are told, its flavor steadily intensifying.

Given what happens to my stomach on the second and third day, the tunta must have been 500 years old.

I observe that the number of mannequins in La Paz must be a healthy percentage of the total human population! From the stores along the Street of Coats, the Street of Weddings, the Street of Flowers, the Street of Hardware, the Street of Shoes, the Street of

---

[4] *Kreis*: a select and secretive circle of writers led by a charismatic figure. The term is generally associated with Stefan George's group in late nineteenth-century, early twentieth-century Germany. In contemporary times the term has been used in association with the 1960s Jack Spicer circle in San Francisco.

Figure 8. Image of Saenz in an *aparapita's* coat

Cloth (La Paz must certainly be the most eighteenth-century Paris–like city on Earth), the mannequins stare out, wacky, grimaced looks right out of late-night shows on the Cartoon Channel. Where do they come from? Is there a Street of Mannequins where one goes to buy them?

All day there are lines by Plaza San Pedro and on Illampu Street where *hechiceros*, seated on small wooden stools and holding frying pans over braziers, melt lead, *plomo*, into a brilliant silver-white liquid that supplicants ladle into a bucket of cold water. Immediately, the lead solidifies into grotesque shapes that tell the future for those who have faith. Here is the alchemist's dream, the lead of spirit transformed into a luminous and malleable promise.

We go, on our last day, to the store of the aged Doña Chepa, one of the most legendary proprietors on Linares. The day before, amidst horns and antlers from apocryphal animals and skins from real jaguar, anaconda, and boar poached from the Beni and Madidi National Parks, I had seen a single condor wing for sale, at least five feet from severed base to tip, stretched out above the age-stained print of an Aryan Jesus. It has been sold. Piled and scattered about are the ubiquitous pink and green holy candies (were these the ones Saenz sucked his teeth out on?), llama fetuses, and dark coprolite-looking things, the identity of which we never do learn.

"And the anaconda skin, how much is it, Doña?"

"Five hundred and fifty, my love."

"Five hundred and fifty bolivianos?"

"No, no, five hundred and fifty dollars. In Miami it would be at least three times that! Skins this size now are very, very rare! Look, if you rolled it out it would reach down to Sagarnaga Street!"

We walk along Avenue Ecuador and, glancing to our right between buildings, see all the way across the city to the far cliffs of La Paz, lit up this early evening in countless yellow, blue, and white speckles of light, a pointillist shimmer.

Accounts of the Poet

We have dinner with the wonderfully kind and brilliant Vicky Ayllon, director of the CEDOAL, and with the country's most famous actor, David Mondaca, who has been making a film about Jaime Saenz. As fireworks celebrating the Festival of San Juan explode over the city sprawling beyond the restaurant's tinted window, he alternately talks about Saenz and impersonates him. His face concentrates and breaks into what can only be called a radiance. Each time he says "Jaime," his voice drops a register and he allows a drag between the syllables to lengthen the name and give it weight.

It's not only his voice. His whole face drops away into something other. It is an astonishing, somewhat disturbing, thing. David and Vicky tell us how his one-man play about Saenz has been a success in numerous countries in Latin America and Europe. But what pleases him most of all is the reception when it is performed in the working class theaters of El Alto, the ramshackle city above La Paz. "The audience feels Jaime as one of them," he says. "It is magic. This is when I have felt the most fulfilled in my life as an artist."

He tells us that Jaime was always sucking mint or caramel candies that, eventually, rotted his teeth. He could have had them fixed, of course, but he was more terrified of dentists than he was of losing his teeth.

We learn that cocaine came to replace alcohol, after he stopped drinking in the mid-'60s. And his consumption of coke is legendary. Saenz began to take it through prescription for a severe toothache, apparently, a very fine strain dispensed by La Paz pharmacies into the early 1980s, according to Blanca. And coke was the drug of choice, too, at the Talleres Krupp. Saenz's principal acolyte, Guillermo Bedregal Garcia, the Rimbaud of Bolivia, who published an astounding body of work before his death at the age of 20 in 1974 (a death he uncannily foretold in two poems), was also an addict. I learn this from his lovely widow, Corina, who at a party toward the end of our stay, tells me, in a voice that makes me think of a music box, all about her young genius husband, and she holds my hand the whole time, as if to comfort me. "Yes, my Guillermo and Jaime used

Figure 9. Experimental photos at the Krupp Workshop

to do coke in large quantities, this was what they did, and then they would talk and write and argue at their voice-tops for days on end! They were so sweet together. Oh, they loved each other like father and son."

Jaime was *el hijo de Illimani*, continues David Mondaca, he was the son of that colossal mountain which presides over La Paz. Also, he was a magic man, *era brujo*. David thoughtfully pulls the end of an imaginary mustache with his thumb and forefinger, and then he draws his palms together over his mouth, praying hands channeling a secret prayer. And a voice comes through him but from somewhere else. It is a swallowed voice, a voice from inside a well, the voice of someone without teeth, of someone whose tongue can't quite get out of breath's way. His words are banked into his inner cheek. They are all but effaced of their distinct phonemes before they finally erupt as the rolling growl of Jaime Saenz.

And after finishing the filming of a scene in the Poet's House, where Saenz last lived, David tells us he stepped outside with the crew, cameras off, and there in front of the house, at that exact moment, passed a "trotting funeral," men high-stepping along the sidewalk with a coffin on their shoulders.

It was a funeral for one of the *aparapita*, the selfless, heroic, hopeless, and stoic caste of men who for centuries have carried great loads up and down the long, steep hills of La Paz. Their creed: They are condemned, and alcohol is their first principle and solace. Three steps out of our hotel, passing the ancient, small church, "at that exact moment," we see an elderly *chola* in elegant *pollera* and shawl, offering her hand to the family members of the deceased, who wait on the steps in greeting line. She is the very first in a long line of condolence behind her. What timing: we are on our way to the CEDOAL, to speak of translating Saenz.

Jaime Saenz's niece, Gisela, remembers his vivid long stories, his descriptions of his walks through the streets she was too young to explore on her own. She remembers the way he held forth in the living room and dominated the conversation.

Something shattered once, Gisela continues. Something broke in the kitchen and the loud noise triggered in her uncle a sudden rage and a tirade she has never forgotten.

Her mother, Jaime's sister, Sra. Elva Morales, puts down her spoon, nods, adds that these moments were often simply "spectacular with drama." But also, she continues, almost at a whisper, there was in him deep tenderness and a great capacity for sympathy. He was a very, very complicated man, she says, looking up, her eyes very wide.

He was known for the vehemence of his assertions. In a book about the places and people of La Paz, Saenz wrote, "Those who do and say things without feeling them, I condemn them a million times."

At lunch one afternoon, Luis Antezana tells us Saenz was "*un hombre*." And here, Luis puts his index finger below his right eye and pulls the flesh down from his lower lid. "*Un hombre muy sabio*." A man very shrewd.

Placing a finger beneath the eye and pulling down the lower lid is also a universal sign of warning or danger in Latin America: the *ojo*. That may be what Luis means, actually: Be careful where you allow him to take you.

Antezana points out that although Saenz always felt a deep empathy and connection with marginalized people, he never romanticized the Aymara. In his writing, Saenz doesn't depict them in indigenous ponchos, but in ragged coats, one part of a vibrant urban collage. Improvising a neologism, Antezana says Saenz *aparapitó* the Aymara, he carried them, in his work, into the pile of life that characterizes the magical hybrid culture of La Paz.

Last Day in La Paz

We learn our first Aymara expression: If you have to lay down your life, you do it.

Figure 10. Jaime and his sister Elva as children

The aparapita with his cargo, ten times larger than himself, running uphill past us, almost brushing us with his load, his eyes glazed, doesn't even glance our way, though here we are, gringos, sticking out like baboons at a baptism. He trots up the cobblestoned street, his dark cheeks almost Dizzy Gillespied with coca leaves. He goes up and up. We walk down, "fresh and rosy," as Saenz says in *To Cross This Distance*, from our "thousand vitamins." Then we go back to the hotel, sit in the flowered courtyard and puff up our cheeks with some just-bought leaves ourselves—we, aging turistas, talking post-

Figure 11. Condor over the Inca Road at the summit of Inka-Rakay

modern poetics, swallowing the juice of the poor. The winter sun feels good on our hamster-like jowls.

Gisela invites us into the room where Saenz's sister has stored his things. We sit at Jaime's wooden writing table upon which she has placed, and covered with a red scarf, his death mask. We try to look elsewhere. Here is a round stain on the table where tea sloshed from its saucer. And here is a cluster of cigarette burns. And here the whole corner must have caught fire. And here, in front, is the little drawer where, in his poem, the night is kept. Gisela plays a tape of Saenz talking in that hollow, smoky voice of his, and we listen and make small talk for an hour, the death mask still veiled before us.

Meanwhile, the centerpiece of his eccentric menagerie, Saenz's famous porcelain doll, huge and life-like, with real blonde hair, gazes at us, bug-eyed in the corner. On the wall, facing us, an imposing painting in gilded frame, circa early eighteenth century, the Virgin Mary levitating, surrounded by cherubs. "Yes," says Gisela, matter-of-factly, "this has been in the family for generations." Sra. Elva comes in cheerily with a plate of sausages and cheeses. "This sausage is a special one—it was Jaime's favorite until he lost his teeth!" Gisela clicks off the tape and smiles at us, coyly. "Well, then. Would you like to see him, finally?" The doll looks on.

As we say goodbye, across the table, over the death mask, dramatically unveiled at last, I notice a pin-prick hole in each of his nostrils.

At dawn, on the way to the airport, our taxi driver takes both hands off the wheel and extends them laterally, one arm out the window, one sweeping into the passenger seat, and then leans sideways in one direction and then the other as he speeds along the highway showing us, frozen in the back seat, how condors fly.

I. La Noche

—A mi dilecto amigo Carlos Alfredo Rivera

I. The Night

—To my beloved friend Carlos Alfredo Rivera

1.

La noche con unos cuernos que se mueven a lo lejos

la noche encerrada en una caja que se vuelve noche en aquella cómoda en el rincón del cuarto

mientras que mis ojos y sobre todo el espacio entre mis ojos y mis narices se transforma a lo largo de una canaleta de dos pisos

me extraña y me causa susto el que haya aparecido un tubo de felpa que se extiende de ojo a ojo y que no me deja ver la noche sino de un modo confuso y fantasmagórico

por obra de una fuerza que ha venido quién sabe de dónde el espacio de mi sueño ha sido dividido por una pared

en este lado no es posible dormir y en el otro lado es perfectamente posible pero no obstante absolutamente imposible

la pared en realidad no es una pared sino una cosa viva que retuerce y palpita y esta pared soy yo

con una transparencia nunca vista que me permite mirar lo que ocurre en el otro lado de la noche

con unos espacios en que seguramente se puede dormir al abrigo de los suspiros interminables y dolidos y de los terrores que se alojan en tus huesos y que te causan mucha congoja

1.

The night, its feelers twitching in the distance

the night locked into a box swallowed by the night in the dresser in the nook

while my eyes and especially that space between my eyes and nostrils stretches out like a two-story gutter

startled and unnerved, I'm suddenly aware—there's a tubular cocoon, spun from eye to eye, through which I see only the night, fractured and phantasmagoric

thanks to a force from who knows where the space of my dream has been split by a wall

on this side sleep is not possible and on the other it's perfectly possible but nevertheless thoroughly impossible

the wall, in fact, is not a wall but a living force that writhes and throbs and this wall is me

with an inconceivable transparency that allows me to see the night's other side

and places you might sleep in an overcoat of aches and interminable sighs and grief-belching terrors which home in on your bones

el otro lado de la noche es una noche sin noche, sin tierra, sin casas, sin cuartos, sin muebles, sin gente

no hay absolutamente nada en el otro lado de la noche,

es un mundo sin mundo por completo y para posesionarse de él será necesario no poder alcanzarlo

—está a la vera de tu cuerpo

y está al mismo tiempo a una distancia inimaginable de él.

the other side of night is a night without night, without earth, without shelter, without rooms, without furniture, unpeopled

there is absolutely nothing on the other side of the night

it's a world utterly without world, and to posess it, you must never arrive there

—it's the dock at the very side of your body

and, at the same time, it's inconceivably remote.

2.

A través de los cables de alta tensión que se extienden en el perfil de las colinas y que luego descienden hacia los campos

la noche se difunde con invisibles chispas que a ratos relampaguean en los ojos y en los botones de algunos vecinos que todavía no se han acostado

y que permanecen valerosamente en las puertas de sus casas para presenciar la primera embestida de la noche.

Esta primera embestida tiene en realidad un origen misterioso,

y sin duda surge de los muertos que han muerto en aras del alcohol y que ahora deliran con la visión que les ofrece el otro lado de la noche,

y tiene mucho que ver con los barriles, con los toneles, con las bodegas, y con los ingentes tanques de alcohol con que sueñan noche tras noche unos bebedores que sólo yo conozco,

y que, habiendo bebido toda su vida hasta reventar, se retuercen en medio de atroces malestares en húmedos camastros y en profundas cloacas pidiendo alcohol a gritos.

Estos bebedores han aprendido muchas cosas y tienen mucha paciencia,

y saben que el otro lado de la noche se halla en el interior de sus espaldas,

2.

Through the high-tension cables which trace the contour of the hills and then plunge to the fields

the night broadcasts itself in invisible sparks that flicker here, now there in the eyes and buttons of neighbors not yet taken by sleep

and who valorously stay fixed to the doors of their dwellings to witness the first onslaught of the night.

This first onslaught has, in truth, a mysterious source,

and no doubt it spurts up from the dead who have died for the sake of alcohol and who now swoon and babble at the vision dangled before them by the other side of the night,

and this has to do with the casks, the kegs, the bars, and the huge vats of alcohol dreamed each and every night by drunks known only to me,

and who, having drunk their whole lives to the seams, writhe, screaming for alcohol, in atrocious spasms on soaked beds and in deep cloacae.

These drunks have learned plenty and they've got patience,

and know the other side of the night has sunk itself into the shaft of their spines,

y que se halla asimismo en sus gargueros,

los cuales conservan siempre un resabio de alcohol,

lo que precisamente tiene la virtud de atormentarlos sin cesar durante el largo, largo tiempo que dura la noche en el otro lado de la noche.

and gone down in their throats,

which retain forever the redolence of alcohol,

which is exactly what torments them unrelentingly,
through the long, long hours of the night on the other side of
the night.

3.

En realidad, el otro lado de la noche es un dominio sumamente extraño,

y es el alcohol quien lo ha creado.

Nadie puede pasar al otro lado de la noche;

el otro lado de la noche es una región prohibida, y sólo podrán entrar en ella los sentenciados.

¿En qué consiste el otro lado de la noche?

El otro lado de la noche consiste en que la noche, simple y llanamente,

se te entra por la espalda y se posesiona de tus ojos, para mirar con ellos lo que no puede mirar con los suyos.

Entonces ocurre una cosa muy rara:

en determinado momento, tú empiezas a mirar el otro lado de la noche,

y muy pronto llegas a comprender que éste se halla ya dentro de ti.

Mas esto, por supuesto, es algo que sólo se da en los grandes bebedores.

3.

Actually, the other side of the night is a supremely esoteric realm,

and alcohol has conjured it.

Not anyone can pass to the other side of the night;

the other side of the night is a forbidden dominion, and only the condemned enter there.

What is the nature of the night's other side?

To put it bluntly, it is the nature of the night's other side

to sink into your spine and colonize your eyes, to see through them what it can't see on its own.

And then a very odd thing happens:

at a certain moment you begin to see the other side of the night,

and you realize with a start it is already inside you.

But this, of course, happens only with the great drunks.

Es privativo de los bebedores que, por haber bebido y bebido sin piedad, han estado muchas veces a un pelo de la muerte.

Es cosa que sólo ocurre con los bebedores que han enloquecido a causa del alcohol.

Con los que no pueden estar un minuto sin beber.

Con los que deciden acortar al máximo las horas de sueño—digamos a dos horas—, a fin de tener más tiempo para beber.

Con los que no ven la hora de estallar de una vez con el alcohol, y que se regodean al sólo pensar en ello.

Con esos.

Sólo a esos el alcohol les concede la gracia de sumergirse para siempre en el otro lado de la noche.

It's exclusive to those who, having pitilessly drunk and drunk, have come, many times, within a hair's breadth of death.

It's something that just comes down on drunks demented by alcohol.

With those who can't go a minute without drinking.

With those who cut their sleep to a dram—two hours let's say—to concoct more time to drink.

With those whose eyes go white at the thought of being blown apart by alcohol.

With those.

Only on those will alcohol confer the grace of everlasting baptism on the other side of the night.

4.

La experiencia más dolorosa, la más triste y aterradora que imaginarse pueda,

es sin duda la experiencia del alcohol.

Y está al alcance de cualquier mortal.

Abre muchas puertas.

Es un verdadero camino de conocimiento, quizá el más humano, aunque peligroso en extremo.

Y tan atroz y temible se muestra, en un recorrido de espanto y de miseria,

que uno quisiera quedarse muerto allá.

Pues el retorno del otro lado de la noche es en realidad un milagro,

y únicamente los predestinados lo logran.

A tu retorno, el mundo te mira con malos ojos:

eres un extraño, eres un intruso, y sientes en lo hondo que el mundo no quiere que lo contemples;

lo que quiere es que te vayas y desaparezcas—lo que quiere es que ya no estés aquí.

4.

The most painful, the most morbid and terrifying experience imaginable

comes by grace of alcohol.

And any walking stiff who wants it can get it.

It opens door after door.

It's an authentic path to knowledge, perhaps the most human of all, though perilous in extremis.

And it shows itself to be so appalling, so inimical, its journey of rue and anguish,

that most would choose to stay on in death.

For any return from the other side of the night is sheer miracle.

And only the chosen accomplish it.

On your return, the world glares at you with malevolent eyes:

you are a stranger, an interloper, and you feel down to your bones how the world abhors your gaze;

what it wants is for you to wane and disappear—what it wants is your absence.

Y como al fin y al cabo el mundo eres tú,

imagínate, tendrás que tener mucha fuerza, mucha
humildad, mucho gobierno,

para enfrentarte contigo mismo

—vale decir, con el mundo.

And since, all in all, you are the world,

do you see, you'll have to be very stalwart, very humble,
very composed,

to face yourself

—which is to say, to face the world.

5.

Luego la noche vendrá en tu ayuda

—y tan sólo ahora, a la luz de experiencias aterradoras
recientemente vividas,

te serán reveladas muchas cosas simples, al par que difíciles.

Pues si no hay riesgo, si no hay peligro, si no hay dolor y
locura,

no hay nada.

El día es para respirar, para saludar, para recorrer muebles
y cambiar de sitio algunas cosas;

el día es de oficinas, de dimes y diretes y de gente buena y
optimista,

y también de pequeños odios y de carreras de velocidad, a
ver quién llega primero.

El día es la superficie del mundo.

La noche no.

La noche es la noche.

La noche, en las profundidades, ha imaginado una broma
pesada—pues la noche escribe,

5.

Later on, the night will rush to help you

—and just then, in the light of all that shook you,

many things will be revealed, simple and also intricate.

For if there is no risk, no peril, if there is no twinge and insanity,

there is nothing.

The day is for breathing, for hellos, for hauling furniture around and rearranging details;

the day of offices, of tell-me's and tell-you's and of placid optimists,

and also of little loathings and full-tilt races to see who arrives first.

The day is the carapace of the world.

Not the night.

The night is the night.

The night, in the deepnesses, has had the last laugh—because the night writes

para buscar y encontrar.

La noche propicia para perderse y desaparecer, para renacer y morir, en oscuridades que te hablan y te señalan.

Por eso la luz de la noche es una luz aparte: muchas cosas, muy extrañas,

se iluminan a la luz de la noche

—las cosas vuelven a ser como lo que son, y uno mismo llega a ser como lo que es.

in order to search and seize.

The night lends itself to loss and disappearance, the better to be reborn and die in darknesses that signal and address you.

So the night's light is a light apart: many and curious things

are lit up by night's light

—things go back to being what they are, and you come to be what you are.

6.

Nadie podrá acercarse a la noche y acometer la tarea de conocerla,

sin antes haberse sumergido en los horrores del alcohol.

El alcohol, en efecto, abre la puerta de la noche; la noche es un recinto hermético y secreto,

que se hunde en lo hondo de los mundos,

y no se podrá mirar en sus adentros, sino por la vía del terror y del espanto.

Además, existen ciertas afinidades con lo oscuro; y quien no las tiene, jamás podrá acercarse a la noche.

Tales afinidades prosperan bajo un signo que podría parecer inconsistente al no iniciado;

pero este signo es ya de por sí indicativo, y lo constituye un extraño y permanente temor de caer en el camino.

De ahí que el iniciado en los secretos de la noche, camine siempre con cautela,

como si de súbito hubiera enceguecido, o hubiera perdido la noción del espacio.

Y es éste en realidad un caminar en las tinieblas

—es de hecho un caminar en el seno de la noche.

6.

No one can near the night and undertake the labor of knowing it

without first immersing himself in the horrors of alcohol.

Alcohol, in fact, opens the night's gates; the night, a secret and hermetic cell

sunk in the suckhole of worlds,

and its bowels can't be seen, but in panic and trembling.

Also, there are certain affinities with darkness, and those who lack them can't near the night.

Such affinities flourish under a sign that might seem contradictory to the uninitiated;

but this sign indicates by its nature, and a queer and unending dread of falling-by-the-wayside holds it together.

Thus an initiate in the night's secrets walks with a ginger step,

as if suddenly struck blind or snapped off from any sense of space.

And this is truly a walk through the umbrae

—is, in effect, a walk through the night's womb.

Pues el iniciado habrá perdido la luz para siempre,

aunque, por otra parte, podrá encontrarla el momento que lo desée,

dispuesto como está a pagar el alto precio que se le exige.

Pues para el hombre que mora en la noche; para aquel que se ha adentrado en la noche y conoce las profundidades de la noche,

el alcohol es la luz.

El que su cuerpo se vuelva transparente, y el que esta transparencia le permita mirar el otro lado de la noche,

es obra exclusiva del alcohol.

For an initiate will have lost the light forever,

although, on the other hand, he can find it when he wants,

ready as he is to pay its high price.

Because for whosoever dwells in the night; for whosoever enters the night and grows acquainted with the profundities of the night,

alcohol is light.

That his body turns transparent, that this transparency grants a vision of the other side of the night,

is due entirely to alcohol.

7.

El que todavía siga habiendo eso que yo llamo la noche, y
el que todavía uno pueda mirarla cuando le da la gana,

es un verdadero milagro

—es algo que yo francamente no alcanzo a explicarme.

Dado el estado del mundo, uno tendría que verse obligado
a trepar a la punta del cerro a ver si encuentra la noche.

Sencillamente, resulta sorprendente que hasta el momento
la noche no haya sido eliminada de la faz del planeta;

liquidada y abolida para siempre, en aras del progreso de la
humanidad y para mayor gloria de la tecnología;

en procura de soluciones radicales para extirpar el mito y la
fantasía,

así como también para que la gente trabaje más y no
duerma tanto.

Capaz que en una de esas le inyecten a la noche unas
cápsulas de láser y le endosen quién sabe qué artefactos de
cobalto, para que cumpla una función verdaderamente útil.

Y te diré que no está lejano el día.

La noche pasará a la historia, y será como la historia del
Arca de Noé y de la Torre de Babel,

7.

That what I call the night goes on, and that you can still check it when you want to,

is a veritable miracle

—it's something I frankly can't explain.

Given the world as it is, you would have to climb cliffs of fall to find the night.

Truth told, it's astonishing the night hasn't been wiped from the planet's face;

slain and vanquished forever, on the altars of human progress and to the greater glory of technology;

in search of radical methods for deracinating myth and the imaginary,

and also so that people work harder and sleep less.

One of these days, no doubt, they'll make the night really useful, zapping it with lasers and dosing it with some kind of cobalt devices.

And I'll tell you the day isn't long in coming.

The night will drift off in history, and it will be like the story of Noah's Ark or the Tower of Babel,

siempre que la tarea no les resulte demasiado difícil y quizá imposible, aun a los propios tecnólogos.

¿A quién irías a quejarte, si un día de esos amaneces y te notifican que ya nunca más habrá noche?

Ante tan tristes perspectivas, es cosa de vida o muerte adoptar extremas decisiones.

Lo primero será adentrarse en la espesura de la noche, para siempre jamás.

Si destruyen la noche, ya no te importa;

el espacio de la noche que tú ocupas, seguirá siendo la noche; será *tú noche*, en un espacio indestructible.

Pues todo se destruye; absolutamente todo. Pero el espacio, es indestructible.

so long as the challenge doesn't prove formidable, insurmountable even to the technicians.

With whom would you file complaint, if one of these days you wake to learn there will be no more night?

Before such morbid prospects, from extreme choices, life and death dangle.

The first step will be to plunge into the pelt of the night without glancing back.

If they obliterate the night, it wouldn't bother you;

the space in the night you occupy will go on being the night; it will be *your night*, an inviolable space.

For all things crumble; absolutely everything. But space, space can't be breached.

8.

Cuando hablo de júbilo y de angustia, me refiero al aprendizaje; y me refiero al conocimiento.

En realidad, me refiero al aprendizaje del conocimiento;

pues una cosa es cierta: no se puede conocer, sin antes haber aprendido a conocer.

Y aprender a conocer no es cosa fácil: duele el cuerpo, duele aquí y duele allá, y duele todo.

Un indefinible malestar se posesiona de ti, y tu cuerpo no es ya el tuyo; es una cosa extraña y ajena.

Y es como una carga que te hubieran impuesto, y que tienes que sobrellevar. Así tus ojos. Así tu lengua. Así tu cabeza. Así tú, todo tú.

Una llamarada de terror y de congoja recorre incesantemente tu cuerpo—y eso que tu cuerpo está lejos, muy lejos.

¿Por qué no puedes moverte?

Se diría que no es ya tu cuerpo. Se diría un túmulo allá, en el camino, sin sol, sin aire y sin agua.

Hay que aprender a comprender lo incomprensible; nadie puede explicártelo.

8.

When I speak of jubilation and anguish, I mean apprenticeship; and I mean intimate knowledge.

Actually, I mean apprenticeship to intimate knowledge;

because one thing is certain: it's not possible to know without first learning to know intimately.

And apprehending intimate knowledge is no easy thing: the body aches with it, it throbs here and throbs again, throbs all over.

A vague malaise grips you, and your body is no longer your own; it is a foreign thing and other.

And it's like a burden they've loaded on you and you've had to accept. So your eyes. So your tongue. So your head. So you, all of you.

A blaze of terror and atrabilium shoots through your body—no matter that your body is far, far away.

What pins you in place?

You might say it's not your body anymore. You might call it a crypt there by the road, sunless, airless, waterless.

It's time to learn to comprehend the incomprehensible; no one can explain it for you.

Tienes que *aprender* tu cuerpo. Y tu cuerpo, a su vez, tiene que *aprender*.

Poco a poco, a lo largo de interminables días y noches, comienzas a aprender.

De hecho, surge una cuestión, absolutamente importante: tienes que tener humor, y tienes que tener aplomo.

Pues deberás mirar de reojo—nunca de frente. No podrías.

El que hubieras estado toda tu vida en contiguidad con la muerte no te sirve de nada,

y sólo te infunde una falsa seguridad y te pierde,

en momentos de supremo terror, que son momentos decisivos en el aprendizaje,

cuando miras de cerca la muerte y cuando de pronto la identificas físicamente y ves la clase de persona que es,

en momentos que precisamente no existe defensa ninguna, como no sea el humor y el aplomo.

Pues la muerte es de carne y hueso,

y conviene recordar que, ello no obstante, nada le impide ocultarse a tus ojos, y asumir formas engañosas y diversas,

mientras juega el simple juego de la muerte, que principia en ti y que termina en mí.

You have to *apprehend* your body. And your body, in turn, has to *apprehend*.

Little by little, in the wake of interminable days and nights, you start to apprehend.

Actually an issue comes up, and it's crucial: you need a sense of humor, and composure.

Because you'll have to look sidewise, never dead-on. You couldn't, anyway.

That you've spent your whole life by the dock of death isn't worth spit,

and only infuses you with false security and loses you

in those moments rife with angst which are the key moments of apprehension,

as when staring at death close-up, and identifying its body, and seeing it for the person it is,

at precisely those moments your defenses thin out, save for some wit and resolve.

For death is flesh and bone,

and you do well to remember, nothing keeps it from giving you the slip, from flaunting myriad, bogus forms,

while it plays, all the while, at death's little game, which begins in you and ends in me.

✺   ✺   ✺

¿Qué es ese peso de angustia, de caída y de perdición que te oprime?

¿Por qué el mundo y las cosas del mundo te causan una pena tan honda?

¿Por qué te resistes a llorar, cuando te acometen infinitas ansias de llorar?

Alguien hurga en tus entrañas.

Alguien respira con aliento lejano—alguien a tu lado.

Mira de reojo. Allá está, vigilante. Muy cerca de ti, con un soplo.

Es algo extremadamente misterioso. Es una persona, yo sé.

Pero no. No es una persona.

Mira de reojo, con cierto disimulo; ella, la persona.

Y te conoce: no eres tú.

Es una silla, es una mesa, una frazada.

Y es una ventana, es un aire, una pared, un moscardón, que vuela en noviembre.

What is this burden of anguish, of loss and perdition that wracks you?

Why do the world and all the world's things fill you with unfathomable woe?

Why do you hold back from weeping when you are seized through and through by the need to weep?

Someone stirs your guts around.

Someone is breathing faintly—someone beside you.

Look sidelong. There, watching you. Very close, a whisper away.

It's an extraordinary riddle. It's a person, I know it.

But no. Not a person.

Looking at you sidelong, with feigned indifference; it, the person.

And it knows you: you are not you.

It's a chair, a table, a blanket.

And it's a window, a breeze, a wall, a blowfly buzzing in November.

Y es una cosa como yo mismo, o como tú, que quizá muere; al igual que yo.

¿Qué será?

Yo no sé, pero la conozco.

And it's a thing just like me, or like you, that perhaps dies, just like me.

What? What?

I don't know, but I know it intimately.

II. El Guardián

II. The Gatekeeper

1.

La montaña con resplandores oscuros en un claro de la noche

con un vestigio de tormenta en algún lugar del tumbado

recordando el dibujo de una taza sin asa más allá del rincón ennegrecido por el humo

con una lata abollada que refleja la manera de mirar y que fatiga y quema los ojos.

La oscuridad interminable en el zócalo que recorre las cuatro paredes de mi cuarto

un poco más arriba del estuco un poco más abajo del empapelado

una raya una señal un amago de luz

una visión que no tiene nada de bueno me asusta y se me erizan los pelos.

Es un hombre encorvado y con ojos relucientes

en el aire espeso y al mismo tiempo translúcido se frota las manos y me mira con pena

1.

   The mountain with sullen radiance in a clearing of the
night

   with a vestige of storm glistening from the sky's vault

   suggesting the sketch of a cup with no handle in the
smoke-mottled corner,

   near a dented tin plate that reflects the gaze and draws
down and stings the eyes.

   The endless dark of the dado rimming my room's four
walls

   a bit above the stucco, a bit below the wallpaper

   a ray a sign a hint of light

   a vile vision sits me bolt upright and stands my hair on end.

   It's a man with humped back and fluorescent eyes

   in thick yet transparent air he rubs his hands and looks at
me, all sorry-eyed

es un hombre alto y usa cuello almidonado y corbata de fantasía

se saca los zapatos seguramente para no hacer ruido primero el diestro y luego el siniestro

yo lo veo acercarse al lecho en que yazgo pero soy incapaz de escuchar lo que me dice

solamente veo sus labios moverse y moverse pronunciando palabras y palabras que empero no me llegan

me oprime la frente con huesuda y fuerte mano

me da un rodillazo en la barriga y un cabezazo en pleno pecho

me hurga los párpados con ágiles dedos y con afiladas uñas me rasca la barba y me hace cosquillas

ahora se pone imponente máscara para escuchar mi corazón

muy pronto retrocede un paso y frotándose las manos se desvanece entre las sombras

pero olvida sus zapatos los cuales para eterna memoria se quedan en mi cuarto.

he's a tall man in a starched collar, a rhinestone tie

he slips off his shoes, no doubt to pad silently first clockwise then counterclockwise

I watch him approach the bed where I lie, but can't hear him

I see his lips pursing and unpursing around words and words I can't make out

he presses my brow with his strong, bony hand

he knees me in the plexus and head-butts my chest

he jabs at my eyelids with quick fingers and with sharp nails rakes my beard and tickles me under the arms

now he dons a huge, bizarre mask and gives a listen to my heart

abruptly he takes one step back and, rubbing his hands, fades slowly into the shadows

but he forgets his shoes, which linger beyond memory in my room.

2.

Se presenta ahora un pariente lejano, a quien sólo reconozco porque tiene bigote y porque se peina con raya en el centro.

A juzgar por las repetidas venias que hace en una y otra dirección, hay mucha gente en el recinto, aunque yo no la veo.

Y como quiera que a mí no me hace ninguna venia, ni me saluda, ni me dice nada,

no tengo más remedio que creer que ya no existo.

De repente agarra y se acerca a mi cabecera, y de buenas a primeras, me da una bofetada.

Claro que es médico; y en tal virtud, no le faltan razones para abofetearme.

Luego agarra y se pone un mandil blanco, y con gesto desdeñoso, me serrucha sin asco.

Y no contento con eso, saca un puñal y me desgarra las carnes, y me tasajea a su regalado gusto;

y después de arrancarme una masa palpitante, picante y vibrante, que parece ser mi estómago,

hunde tamaño cuchillo en mis verijas, y por poco no me corta las huevas.

Y con esto, hace repetidas venias, y se aleja.

2.

Who shows up now but a distant cousin I only recognize by his mustache, his oily hair parted up the middle.

From his polite little nods in this and that direction, you might imagine the room full of people, but I don't see them.

And noting that he doesn't nod politely in my direction, nor glance at me, nor say a word to me,

I can only assume I no longer exist.

Suddenly he grabs my headboard, yanks himself close, and right off the bat, he smacks me silly.

Of course, he must be a doctor and must have his reasons.

Then snatching and knotting a butcher's apron, smirking contemptuously, he hacks at me with a saw, full of gusto,

and because he hasn't had enough, he whips out a carving knife and disembowels me and whisks my entrails with undisguised relish,

and after yanking out a steaming, live, throbbing mass that would seem to be my stomach,

he plunges the great blade into my groin, missing my balls by a hair.

And with this, he backs away, nodding politely.

3.

¿Quién es ése, con cuello de toro y melena de león?

Aparece en este instante ante la puerta, cual guardián del umbral, y no deja pasar a nadie.

Hay sol, hay agua, hay respiración en los aires,

y también hay gente.

Un murmullo de seres que vuelan y vuelan y vuelan se percibe en la atmósfera.

Y este murmullo, que de pronto resuena en todos los ámbitos, y que se torna y en estruendo,

es sin embargo un silencio más hondo que el propio silencio.

Hay dos mundos, hay dos vidas, hay dos muertes

—eso que llaman lo uno y absoluto, no existe.

Hay dos caras, dos filos, dos abismos.

El guardián se fatiga.

Ya no puede más con el sol, y lanza miradas amenazadoras a la gente que pugna por entrar a verme.

3.

Who is that, the one with bull's neck and lion's mane?

He appears from nowhere in the doorway, this gatekeeper of the threshold, blocking those who would pass through.

There is sunlight, and water, and air heavy with beathing,

and there are people.

The air hums with the fluttering and fluttering and fluttering of beings.

And this humming, which resounds in every realm, rising to a roar,

is nevertheless a silence more profound than pure silence.

There are two worlds, there are two lives, there are two deaths,

—whatever they call the One and Absolute doesn't exist.

There are two faces, two edges, two abysses.

The gatekeeper wearies.

The sun has gotten to him, and with glowering eyes he cuts down those who clamor to come in and see me.

El Facundo, un buen carpintero, le presta un sombrero de paja. La señora Anselma le ofrece un vaso de agua.

Un señor, de recia carita, le da un cigarrillo, y murmura algo en su oído.

El guardián entrecierra los ojos, como un soñador; cruza los brazos sobre el pecho, con aire imponente;

y de rato en rato, saca un reloj de su bolsillo y consulta la hora,

y luego mira el cielo.

Mas en una de esas, lanza un grito de espanto, y se queda como petrificado.

Pues habiendo aparecido en estos precisos momentos una mariposa nocturna,

tan negra como la noche,

en pleno día y bajo un sol radiante,

con una orla de color morado en las enormes alas, batiendo éstas con extraña lentitud,

describe un círculo, y desciende poco a poco;

y de pronto se posa en la frente del aterrado guardián,

Facundo, the good carpenter, lends him a straw fedora.
Señora Anselma offers him a glass of water.

A man with a grim brow gives him a cigarette and whispers in his ear.

The gatekeeper, like a dreamer, half-closes his eyes and folds his arms defiantly across his chest,

and every so often consults his pocket watch,

and then stares at the sky.

But in the middle of this casual regime he shrieks and stiffens.

For a night moth has suddenly appeared,

black as night,

in the middle of the day in clear sun,

with a fringe of purple on its enormous wings, flapping with weird torpor,

tracing a spiral that slowly descends;

and it settles on the brow of the terrified gatekeeper,

y allí se queda, para eterna memoria;

como estampada en una tela, o como labrada a fuego en el yelmo de legendario caballero.

and there it stays, beyond memory,

as if stamped in cloth, or forged by fire into the shield of a mythical knight.

4.

Este pobre cuerpo, abandonado;

este pobre cuerpo, ido y botado, y bastante olvidado, con una presencia que sólo se deja presentir por la pesantez,

y con patas como palos aquí, y con brazos ardientes y paralizados allá

—ahora no existen ya esos olores extraños y desconocidos, y aun inventados, que te llevaban a los mundos que precisamente querías habitar.

Ahora los olores no son ya sino olores, en toda su verdad,

y sólo pertenecen a tu cuerpo, y corresponden a tu condición humana.

¿Acaso pretendías oler a rosas o a madreselvas, o a ramas de pino,

para que ahora te horrorices y aun te sientas ofendido, ante los olores que expiden tus propias excreciones?

El olor, por otra parte, es un verdadero misterio;

y no estará demás recordar que tanto el nacimiento como la muerte, ocurren bajo el signo de peculiares cuanto atroces olores.

4.

This poor, abandoned body;

this poor, squandered body, good as forgotten, situated only by the gravity of its situation,

and with stick legs here, and with baked, stick arms there,

—now those peculiar and unknown smells, even the imagined ones, evaporate, the ones that transported you to the very worlds for which you longed.

Now the smells are nothing but smells, in all their verity,

and they pertain only to your body, your human condition.

Had you hoped to smell like roses, or honeysuckle, or pine boughs,

only to be taken aback, even horrified, by the smell of your own excretions?

Smell, moreover, is a great enigma;

nor is it beside the point to remember that birth as well as death are announced by singular, stunning smells.

5.

¿Cómo aprender a morir?

—ha de ser una cosa en extremo difícil.

Seguramente requiere mucha humildad y mucho gobierno.

Toda una vida de trabajo y de meditación.

Y si uno se pregunta para qué aprender a morir,

la respuesta surge de por sí:

aprender a morir es aprender a vivir.

Y aprender a vivir es, en definitiva, aprender a conocer;

pues no deberá olvidarse que, para conocer, primero habrá que aprender a conocer.

❧   ❧   ❧

En las noches, a lo largo de los años, uno se queda horas y horas, pensando en muchas cosas.

Pero en realidad, uno no se queda pensando muchas cosas; la verdad es que uno se queda, y nada más.

5.

How should you learn to die?

—it must be a bitterly hard thing.

No doubt it requires a lot of humility and self-control.

A whole life of effort and meditation.

And if you ask yourself why learn to die,

the answer comes clear:

learning to die is learning to live.

And learning to live is, plainly, learning to know deep in the bone;

but don't forget that for intimate knowledge, you must first learn how to know deep in the bone.

   ❧   ❧   ❧

At night, through the years, hours and hours are spent thinking.

But you don't really spend time thinking; the truth is that you simply spend the time, and that's all.

Completamente inmóvil, mirando el vacío. Y—¿por qué no decirlo? —uno se pone triste, miserablemente triste.

Y lo que más tristeza causa, es uno mismo—el estar ahí.

Sin saber qué hacer. Sin saber nada de nada.

Y de repente ocurre un milagro:

el rato menos pensado, empieza a llover, y un relámpago te deslumbra—un sentimiento de invulnerabilidad te envuelve,

con la lluvia.

Y si te dan ganas de escribir algún poema evocador, seguramente no lo escribes;

prefieres escuchar la lluvia.

Pues una voz interior te revela que aquel poema evocador se encuentra en tu bolsillo.

Y ésta es cosa que no te causa el menor asombro, acostumbrado como estás a los prodigios:

en efecto, el poema se halla en tu bolsillo; y lo sacas, y lo miras, y lo lees.

Y de pronto te preguntas quién habrá sido su autor,

como si no supieras que aún no ha nacido.

Completely still, eyes on the abyss. And—why not say it—
you get sad, miserably so.

And what makes you saddest is yourself—the being there.

Without knowing what to do. Without knowing anything
about anything.

And from nowhere there's a miracle:

when it's least expected it starts to rain, and a lightning
flash stuns you—you are cloaked in an invulnerability,

with the rain.

And if you get the urge to write some poignant poem, you
probably won't;

you'd rather listen to the rain.

For some voice inside you whispers that the poignant
poem is folded inside your pocket.

And this is something that doesn't surprise you at all,
accustomed as you are to miracles:

indeed, the poem is in your pocket; you take it out and
read it.

And all of a sudden you wonder who the author might be,

as if you had no idea he hasn't yet been born.

6.

A lo largo de los años, tus cosas y tus muebles se envejecen, y se desgastan insensiblemente.

Muchos objetos desaparecen o se rompen, mientras que otros corren una suerte misteriosa, cual si fueran seres humanos.

Un tintero de cristal de roca, que yo veneraba, fue a parar a la policía, en circunstancias extrañas y absurdas;

Una pistola automática se quedó empeñada por largo tiempo en una chingana, y habiendo sido redimida por el Forito Cisneros éste la utilizó para suicidarse.

Por causa de un lente de diez centímetros de diámetro, que en mala hora presté a un profesor, se cometieron varios hechos de sangre.

Unos aparatos de alta diatermia, que producían oscuros resplandores de color violeta, y que estaban empeñados en una botica, fueron recuperados con mi autorización por un conocido mío, quien comenzó a manipular dichos aparatos en forma tan imprudente que cayó fulminado. Actualmente se hallan empeñados en una sastrería, y no pienso recogerlos.

Las *Obras Completas* de Nietzsche, en doce tomos, salieron de mi cuarto una noche, para no volver jamás. Pues las empeñamos a las volandas a un chofer que manejaba un taxi, y, con el entusiasmo, nos olvidamos preguntarle su nombre y anotar el número del auto.

Idéntica cosa ocurrió con una máquina de escribir portátil, que era la niña de mis ojos.

6.

Over the years, all your furniture and possessions wear down and fine away.

Many things disappear or break, while others meet odd fates, as if they were human.

A crystal inkwell I adored wound up with the cops, under totally bizarre circumstances;

an automatic pistol sat pawned in a whorehouse for ages, until Forito Cisneros redeemed it to kill himself.

Thanks to a magnifying glass ten centimeters in diameter which, on a misguided lark, I lent to an academic, a series of bloody atrocities were committed.

Some high-energy apparatuses, which triggered resplendent violet rays, and which were in pawn to an apothecary shop, were redeemed, with my authorization, by an acquaintance who undertook to fool around with said apparatuses in such a manner that he was electrocuted stone-dead. Presently they are pawned to a tailor shop, and I have no intention of redeeming them.

The *Complete Works of Nietzsche*, in twelve volumes, left my room one night, never to return. For we pawned them on a whim to a cab driver, and in our exuberance, forgot to ask his name or take down the license number.

The exact same thing happened with a portable typewriter, the apple of my eye.

Referir el destino de mis cosas sería de nunca acabar.

Lo que me apena es el destino que han corrido, y lo que asimismo me acongoja es el destino que correrán todas aquellas que todavía me acompañan.

Me causa alarma el ver cómo se borran los dibujos tallados en las sillas.

El estado calamitoso de una butaca que, por otra parte, ha de tener ya sus buenos cien años.

Me duele el aspecto que ofrece mi mesa de escribir, totalmente cacarañada y deteriorada, aunque sumamente respetable y fornida.

Un velador más antiguo que mi alma, y que perteneció a mi abuela, ya sin color, tremendamente noble, soportando todos los embates, los golpes, las patadas y las borracheras.

Sin embargo la mesa, hecha en Viena, pequeña y con tapa, de mi madre, está en buen estado, aunque con algunos rasguños.

El estante alto y vertical, de palo de rosa, con una puerta y con pirograbados, que me regaló mi tía Esther, está en su lugar; y si algo me fascina, es el desgaste que ha sufrido.

Por lo demás, hay un mundo de cosas.

Una mesa de ruedas, con dos divisiones, desvencijada; un ropero de nogal, en ruinas; otros muebles, con mucha historia, con mucho misterio, y con una vejez que asusta.

To ledger the fate of my belongings would be endless.

What irks me is the fate they suffered, and what irks me no less is the fate to be suffered by all the stuff I still keep around.

I'm alarmed by the way the designs carved into the seats of my chairs are rubbed out.

The calamitous state of my armchair, which, moreover, must be pushing a hundred years.

The appearance of my writing desk wounds me, all pocked and cigarette-burned, though still solid and noble.

Bequeathed to me by grandmother, a bedside table, older than my soul, now bleached out, clutching its dignity, the survivor of toe-stubs, bumps, kicks, and drunken falls.

Nevertheless, the table, made in Vienna, petite and glass-covered, handed down from mother, is in decent shape save for a few nicks.

The tall, skinny bookcase, made of rosewood, with a door and delicate pyrography, a gift from Aunt Esther, stands in its place; and if anything fascinates me, it's the neglect it has suffered.

Apart from these, there is a whole world of things.

A wheeled table with double leaves, gone rickety; a walnut armoire in ruins; more furniture full of history, and mystery, appallingly antique.

¿Cuánto valdrán estos muebles?—me pregunto yo.

Pues en realidad, no valen nada; y, en el mejor de los casos, capaz que su valor total no alcance para una ranga-ranga.

Son tristes trastos, vejestorios, muebles pasados de moda

—y por idéntica razón, forman parte inseparable de tu vida y te da pena dejarlos.

What's it all worth? I ask myself.

Well, in truth, not much, and even under the best circumstances, not enough to buy a ranga-ranga.

They're all sad pieces of junk, rickety wrecks, long out of style

—and, precisely for that reason, they are indivisible from life, and it's murder to let them go.

7.

¿Cuánto dura la noche?

En realidad nadie sabe, aunque le haya sido asignada una duración de doce horas, por razones de orden puramente práctico.

Lo cierto es que la noche dura en el espacio, mientras que el día sólo dura en el tiempo.

Así se explica el que a toda hora del día, uno encuentre regiones en que la noche mora.

Tales regiones se identifican con el musgo, con el metal, y con el viento;

con un silencio comunicativo, que surge de las piedras, y que se suspende en el vacío.

Tales regiones suelen encontrarse asimismo en algunos rostros, que se nos aparecen fugitivamente por las calles, y que nos transmiten un mensaje.

Las regiones en que mora la noche, en pleno día, se encuentran aquí, en este papel,

y también allá, en el otro papel.

Y se encuentran en muchos lugares, en muchas personas, en muchos animales, y en muchos objetos.

A la primera mirada, y aun por el tacto y por el olor, uno puede reconocer estas regiones.

7.

How long does the night go on?

No one can guess, even if, for purely practical reasons, it's been assigned twelve hours.

The sure thing is that night endures in space, while day takes place purely in time.

That's why at any given time of day you can find regions where the night dwells.

Such regions are signed with moss, metal, and wind;

with a pregnant silence that oozes from the stones and hovers in emptiness.

Such regions are often found, just the same, on certain faces which abruptly appear to us on the streets, disgorging their message.

The regions where the night, in plain day, dwells, are to be found here, on this very paper,

and also over there, on that other paper,

and they are to be found in many places, in many people, in many animals, many objects.

At a glance, even by touch and scent, you can discern these regions.

En un talismán de estaño, por muchos años olvidado en alguna gaveta;

en un sobre de color oscuro, con una inscripción que no se lee ya,

encontrarás una región que habita la noche;

en esas piedras del camino, que parecen esperarte, y parecen mirarte.

En alguna llave, inservible ya, y venida a menos, que se esconde en tu bolsillo;

en esa cicatriz, que ha aparecido sin saberse cómo, en tu mano izquierda

—en alguna concavidad de tu calavera, que muchas veces te escuece sin saberse por qué,

encontrarás una región que habita la noche.

Y la encontrarás en ese rayo de luz, que se filtra por la ventana,

y que alumbra el vuelo del moscardón.

In a tin fetish, long forgotten in a drawer;

in a dark-hued envelope, in a faded inscription,

there you'll come across a region where night dwells;

in those stones along the path, which seem to wait for you, watching you.

In an old and useless key buried in your pocket;

in that scar, from who knows what, on your left hand

—in some crater of your skull, which often burns without warning,

there you'll find a region where the night dwells.

And you'll find it in that sunbeam which the window softens,

and which renders the flight of the blowfly.

III. Intermedio

III. Interval

Sucedió una noche de noviembre.

Angustiosamente y con ojos extraviados me debatía en medio del tormento de cuatro días sin sueño,

cuando de pronto se escucharon atroces alaridos y voces y lamentos que llegaban a mis oídos desde lo hondo de un pozo fatídico,

y que dejaban adivinar horrores sin cuento,

por lo que me invadió el terror y me quedé mudo de espanto,

contemplando silenciosamente inmóviles aguas con una negrura reluciente,

que reflejaban formas fosforescentes de personajes depravados, de multitudes ensangrentadas, de ciudades asoladas, y de seres enloquecidos.

∾∾∾ ∾∾∾ ∾∾∾

Came a night in November.

Tormented and seeing double, I floundered in the wake of four insomniac days,

when unexpectedly, blood-curdling howls and babblings and sobs riveted my ears to the yawn of an ominous hole,

evoking unspeakable foreboding,

impaling me with panic and hissing me mute with fear,

as I looked out on obsidian waters, dead calm and shimmering in blackness,

which reflected phosphorescent silhouettes of depraved, blood-drenched mobs, razed cities and frenzied masses.

❧   ❧   ❧

No había una estrella.

No había un planeta.

No había firmamento—el cielo estaba en tinieblas.

Sin embargo, hacia el norte, una nube reflejaba el resplandor de la ciudad,

y rompía el espeso manto de sombras.

Y extrañamente, en la esquina del Hospital General, en Miraflores, reinaba una oscuridad total y absoluta;

y era ésta una oscuridad ultraterrena, una oscuridad nunca vista.

Y la gente se reunía en las proximidades, guardando una prudente distancia;

y todos dirigían recelosas y asustadas miradas hacia el tenebroso ámbito

—y a ese paso, cundía el pánico.

El caso es que para terror de los habitantes, el grave prodigio persistió por espacio de largos días;

y tan sólo al cabo de una semana se hizo la luz.

Poco después del misterioso suceso—que en adelante se llamaría *la maldición de la esquina*—,

There was not a star.

There was not a planet.

There was no firmament—the sky smudged with gloom.

Nevertheless, in the north, the city's light glowered in a cloud,

and cracked the thick mantle of shadow.

And oddly, at the corner of the General Hospital, on Avenue Miraflores, an absolute and total darkness reigned;

and this darkness was otherworldly, a darkness never seen before.

And people congregated around it, though keeping their distance;

And they all stared transfixed and numb at the umbra

—and then a panic spread.

In fact, to the mounting terror of the populace, the grave event poured itself into many long days;

and only after a whole week did the light snap on again.

Shortly after the bizarre event—which henceforth would be called *The Bewitching of the Corner*—

pavorosos al par que inenarrables desastres se abatieron sobre la población.

Nadie en el mundo podía explicar los acontecimientos que a diario ocurrían;

y era cada vez más difícil controlar a las turbamultas enloquecidas, que se lanzaban a las calles y que provocaban el caos.

En pleno día, el sol se oscurecía, y la ciudad se anegaba en un mar de tinieblas.

Estruendos sobrenaturales atronaban en el seno de la tierra, y muy pronto sobrevenía un silencio de muerte.

Mucha gente, que enloquecía por causa del terror a lo desconocido, se ahorcaba.

Hombres y mujeres, niños y ancianos, incendiaban las casas para procurarse luz,

y saltaban a las llamas y se quemaban vivos.

Al cabo el sol brillaba ya con inusitado resplandor, y con esto, el pánico y la locura subían de punto.

Y así, cada día.

Ora una luz encubridora, ora una oscuridad aterradora, al decir de un poeta que cantaba la catástrofe.

brutal and spectacular disasters rained down on the populace.

Not a soul could explain the weirdness going down every day;

and it was increasingly hard to control the tumultuous mobs, who flung themselves chaotically into the streets.

At the very apex of the day, the sun would blank out, and the whole city sink in a sea of shadows.

Fantastic concussions rang out from the pit of the earth, and presently a funereal silence took hold.

Lots of people, crazed with dread of the unknown, hanged themselves.

Men and women, children and the aged, set fire to buildings for the sake of light,

and then they leaped into the flames, to be roasted alive.

After a while, inexplicably, the sun would emerge blazing its insane brilliance, and with this, the frenzy and madness surged to an uncontrollable pitch.

And so on, day after day.

Now a light ensheathing, now a dark insaning, as a poet, in an ode to the catastrophe, put it.

O el calor resultaba infernal y mortal, o el frío alcanzaba el grado sesenta bajo cero,

con lo que miles de personas y animales aparecían como estatuas de carne y hueso decorando las calles.

Así las cosas, de un tiempo a esta parte, unos negros, monstruosos y gigantescos, y con aire amenazador y brutal,

y con campanillas en las orejas, y con manos blancas como la nieve,

habían aparecido en las calles;

y ya de entrada, habían provocado un terror que sobrepasaba el paroxismo.

El hecho es que estos negros transitaban sin mirar a nadie, muy ensoberbecidos y prepotentes,

en extraños vehículos con esferas en lugar de ruedas, que se deslizaban a gran velocidad,

y que emitían vibraciones maléficas y de alta energía.

Y cuando se hacían las tinieblas, estos vehículos arrojaban resplandores que paralizaban,

y luego producían un rugido que embrutecía y que enloquecía, y que causaba la muerte.

Either the heat was deadly and infernal, or the cold plummeted to a hundred below,

freezing multitudes to the boulevards, statues of flesh and bone.

So things went, and by and by, the dark ones, monstrous and huge, with savage, menacing intensity,

with bells in their ears, and with hands white as snow,

appeared in the streets;

and from the get-go they provoked a general pall that spilled past the bounds of paroxysm.

The fact is, these dark ones cruised along without glancing at anyone, arrogant as lords and cold-hearted,

riding strange machines with spheres for wheels, rolling along at fabulous speeds,

emitting malevolent, charged vibrations.

And when the darkness gathered, these machines shot out brilliant, paralyzing beams,

and roared so viciously, people were driven to madness and death.

Por otra parte, estos negros contaban con verdaderos batallones de esclavos;

y estos esclavos, armados de lanzas y látigos, se desbordaban en todo lo largo y lo ancho de la ciudad,

conduciendo feroces jaurías de mastines,

para arremeter contra indefensas y compactas multitudes, y sembrar el terror y la muerte.

Los negros, con suntuosas vestiduras de raro material, y con ojos que relampagueaban en la oscuridad,

vivían en el mejor de los mundos.

Ocupaban espaciosos palacios de piedra, construidos por los indios, a quienes sometían a sistemáticos tormentos;

celebraban bestiales rituales mensuales, para convocar al Negro Cabruja, y con tal motivo, hacían correr torrentes de sangre;

se daban sabatinos banquetes de carne humana, en una mesa con capacidad para mil negros;

y se abastecían de fabulosos nepentes y manjares, por medio de aviones que, a su paso, lanzaban rayos y truenos sobre la población.

Y así los negros, como quien nada hace, cometían toda clase de atrocidades.

In addition, these dark ones had at their command veritable battalions of slaves;

and these slaves, armed with spears and whips, swept into every nook and cranny of the city,

driving packs of rabid dogs before them,

to assault defenseless, huddled crowds, and to lay waste to everyone and everything.

The dark ones, dressed in ceremonial robes of exotic fabrics, their eyes candescent in the dark,

exulted in the most splendorous of worlds.

They set up in vast stone palaces, built by the Indians, whom they tormented without pause;

they held beastly monthly rituals, summoning the dark Witch-of-Fuck, and at those times, torrents of blood ran;

they held feasts of human flesh on the Sabbath, at a table spread for a thousand of their kind;

and with the aid of flying machines they stocked up on luscious fruits and delicacies, while with these same machines they unleashed lightning and thunder on the people.

And thus the dark ones, as if it were all merely ho-hum, committed every atrocity.

Por lo demás, existían famosos al par que despiadados tecnólogos entre los negros;

y su único oficio era destruir y matar.

Muchas veces practicaban redadas de niños y de jóvenes vigorosos y sanos;

y los acorralaban en inmensos galpones de la aduana, con objeto de incrementar las reservas de carne.

La verdad es que estos negros no eran negros; y ya de hecho, no pertenecían a la raza humana.

Y como no podía ser de otra manera, profesaban la tecnología por toda religión,

y disponían de una asombrosa diversidad de androides, para programar infinitos y monstruosos desvaríos.

Entre broma y broma, planificaron el confinamiento de la población a túneles que se hundirían en lo profundo de la tierra,

y que serían construidos por los propios pobladores;

intentaron repetidas veces la voladura de los cerros circunvecinos, con explosivos atómicos que, por fortuna, no se activaron;

What's more, there were prominent and despicable technophiles among them,

and their one purpose was to devastate and murder.

Often, there were mass round-ups of children and of the most vigorous and healthy adolescents;

and these were corralled into the huge warehouses of the Customs Bureau, augmenting the supply of meat.

In truth, these dark ones were not simply dark ones; they weren't, in fact, human.

And because they couldn't help themselves, they made technology the true god,

and they had at their command a vast array of androids to program extensive, psychotic debaucheries.

Between one joke and another, they planned the entombment of the population in deep tunnels

to be dug by those they would entomb;

they repeatedly attempted to level the surrounding mountain ranges with atomic devices, which, thank goodness, didn't go off;

tenían decidido bombardear ciudades, pueblos y caseríos, para probar el poder destructor de ciertos cohetes nucleares;

y con experimentos demenciales y criminales, por poco no liquidan la flora y la fauna en vastas regiones del Kollao.

🙠   🙠   🙠

Largo sería enumerar los horrores que se dejaban presentir aquella noche de noviembre,

y que se manifestaban bajo la forma de lamentos angustiosos y de gritos desgarradores, que surgían de lo hondo del fatídico pozo,

mientras que inmóviles aguas con una negrura reluciente reflejaban formas siempre fosforescentes.

Lo cierto es que tan horrendas visiones se disiparon poco a poco, y terminaron por desvanecerse como el humo a lo lejos.

they'd already decided to bomb cities, towns, and hamlets, to test the efficacy of various nuclear missiles;

and by means of demented and criminal experiments, they came within a whisper of liquidating all the flora and fauna in the vast territories of the Kollao.

❦   ❦   ❦

It would take too long to relate what was foretold that November night, the horrors

revealed as anguished laments and harrowing screams, drifting up from the depths of the ominous hole,

while obsidian waters, in a dead calm, shimmered with opalescent forms.

Verily, these sickening visions dissipated bit by bit, until they vanished like smoke in the distance.

IV. La Noche

IV. The Night

1.

Extrañamente, la noche en la ciudad, la noche doméstica, la noche oscura;

la noche que se cierne sobre el mundo; la noche que se duerme, y que se sueña, y que se muere; la noche que se mira,

no tiene nada que ver con la noche.

Pues la noche sólo se da en la realidad verdadera, y no todos la perciben.

Es un relámpago providencial que te sacude, y que, en el instante preciso, te señala un espacio en el mundo:

un espacio, uno solo;

para habitar, para estar, para morir—y tal el espacio de tu cuerpo.

1.

Strangely, the night of the city, the domestic night, the obscure night;

the night that circles the world, the night that is slept, and dreamt, the night that is died into, the night that is seen,

has nothing whatever to do with the night.

Because the night only presents itself in the real, and not everyone can perceive it.

It's a providential shiver of light that stuns you, and shows you, in one precise instant, a space inside the world:

a space, one alone;

in which to make a home, to stay, to die—and thus the space of your body.

2.

Pues existe un mandato, que tú deberás cumplir.

en homenaje a la realidad de la noche, que es la tuya propia;

aun a costa de renunciamientos imposibles, y de interminables tormentos,

deberás decir adiós, y recogerte al espacio de tu cuerpo.

Y deberás hacerlo, sin importar el escarnio y la condena de un mundo amable y sensato.

Es de advertir que miles y miles de mortales se recogen tranquilamente al espacio de sus respectivos cuerpos,

día tras día y quieras que no, al toque de rutilantes trompetas, y en medio de lágrimas y lamentos;

pues en realidad, recogerse al espacio del cuerpo, es morir.

Pero aquí no se trata de morir.

Aquí se trata de cumplir el mandato; y por idéntica razón, habrá que vivir.

Y tan es así, que no se podrá cumplir el mandato, sino a condición de recogerse al espacio del cuerpo, con el deliberado propósito de vivir.

2.

For there is a mandate you must obey,

in tribute to the night's truth, which is your truth;

even if at the cost of impossible sacrifices and endless torments,

you must say goodbye and retreat into the space of your body.

And so you must, regardless of the mockery and contempt from a kind and rational world.

Note that thousands on thousands of mortals slip effortlessly into the respective spaces of their bodies,

day after day, like it or not, to the clamor of refulgent trumpets, and at the center of weeping and wailing;

because, truth told, to retreat into the space of the body is to die.

But here we're not talking about dying.

Here we're talking about obeying the mandate; and for that, it shall be necessary to live.

And this is so real that the mandate can't be obeyed but by retreating into the space of the body with the sole purpose of living.

Lo cierto es que aquel que acomete tan alta aventura, no hace otra cosa que ocultarse de la muerte,

para vislumbrar así la manera de ser de la muerte.

It's certain, those who risk such a rare thing disguise
themselves from death,

only to glimpse there death's raison d'être.

3.

El espacio que tu cuerpo ocupa en el mundo, es igual al espacio del cuerpo en el que uno se ha recogido;

y si esto es así, nadie tiene por qué molestarte, ni importunarte;

en el espacio de tu cuerpo, del que tú eres el soberano absoluto,

puedes pararte de cabeza y hacer y deshacer, y transitar tranquilamente,

libre ya de un mundo de pesadilla, poblado de espectros y de esqueletos que pululaban y te quitaban la vida.

En todo caso, tu morada, tu ciudad, tu noche y tu mundo, se reducen a tu cuerpo;

y quien lo habita no eres tú, sino el cuerpo de tu cuerpo.

Pues el cuerpo que te habita, en realidad, eres tú;

Sólo que tu cuerpo deja de ser tú,

y pasa a ser él.

Imagínate, el cuerpo que eres tú, habitando el cuerpo que es él,

y que no por eso deja de ser tú.

3.

The space your body takes up in the world is equal to the space of the body into which someone has retreated;

and, if so, no one has any reason to bother or pester you;

in the space of your body, where you are absolute sovereign,

you can stand on your head, create and decreate, and wander at ease,

free at last of a nightmarish world full of swarming specters and skeletons who siphoned your life.

In any case, your dwelling, your city, your night, and your world boil down to your body;

and the one who dwells there is not you, but the body of your body.

For the body that dwells in you is, in reality, you;

it's only that your body leaves off being you,

and passes into itself.

Imagine: the body that is you dwelling within the body that is itself,

but which, for that, won't cease being you.

De ahí el habitante, o sea, el cuerpo de tu cuerpo; y de ahí, asimismo, el habitado, o sea, tu cuerpo.

¿Y qué decir de la honda soledad, habitando el espacio de tu cuerpo?

Hay un echar de menos la soledad, cuando hay alguien a tu lado;

pero, cuando no hay un alma, es la propia soledad quien te echa de menos

—y es como si tú no estuvieras, o como si te hubieras ido, en busca de alguien a quien echar de menos.

La soledad en el espacio de tu cuerpo, ha de ser, pues, una soledad muy larga, muy alta, y muy álgida

—como esa soledad que uno imaginaba de niño,

con un retrato desaparecido y una rueda inmóvil, en el cuarto oscuro.

Therein the inhabitant, who is the body of your body; therein, likewise, the inhabited one, who is your body.

And what of the illimitable loneliness nestled in the space of your body?

There is a longing for loneliness when someone is by your side;

but with no one there, it is loneliness who longs for you

—and it's as if you weren't there, or as if you had gone away looking for someone else to miss.

The loneliness within the space of your body shall be, then, a protracted one, regal and algid

—like the loneliness you imagined as a child,

a lost portrait and a stilled wheel in the dismal room.

4.

¿Qué es la noche?—uno se pregunta hoy y siempre.

La noche, una revelación no revelada.

Acaso un muerto poderoso y tenaz,

quizá un cuerpo perdido en la propia noche.

En realidad, una hondura, un espacio inimaginable.

Una entidad tenebrosa y sutil, tal vez parecida al cuerpo que te habita,

y que sin duda oculta muchas claves de la noche.

❧   ❧   ❧

Cuando pienso en el misterio de la noche, imagino el misterio de tu cuerpo,

que es sólo una manera de ser de la noche;

yo sé de verdad que el cuerpo que te habita no es sino la oscuridad de tu cuerpo;

y tal oscuridad se difunde bajo el signo de la noche.

En las infinitas concavidades de tu cuerpo, existen infinitos reinos de oscuridad;

4.

What is the night?—you ask now and forever.

The night, a revelation still veiled.

Perhaps a deathform, tenacious and flexed,

perhaps a body lost to the night itself.

Truly, a chasm, a space unimaginable.

A subtle, lightless realm, not unlike the body dwelling in you,

which hides, surely, many clues to the night.

꙯ ꙯ ꙯

When I consider the night's mystery, I imagine the mystery of your body,

which is only one of the forms of night's being;

I know beyond doubt the body that inhabits you is nothing more than the darkness of your body;

and this darkness is diffused under the night's sign.

In the countless concavities of your body there are multiple kingdoms of darkness;

y esto es algo que llama a la meditación.

Este cuerpo, cerrado, secreto y prohibido; este cuerpo, ajeno y temible,

y jamás adivinado, ni presentido.

Y es como un resplandor, o como una sombra:

sólo se deja sentir desde lejos, en lo recóndito, y con una soledad excesiva, que no te pertenece a ti.

Y sólo se deja sentir con un pálpito, con una temperatura, y con un dolor que no te pertenecen a ti.

Si algo me sobrecoge, es la imagen que me imagina, en la distancia;

se escucha una respiración en mis adentros. El cuerpo respira en mis adentros.

La oscuridad me preocupa—la noche del cuerpo me preocupa.

El cuerpo de la noche y la muerte del cuerpo, son cosas que me preocupan.

🌿   🌿   🌿

Y yo me pregunto:

and this is something worth reflection.

This body, closed, secret, and forbidden; this body, other and fearsome,

neither foretold nor foreseen.

And it is like a resplendence or like a shadow:

it only allows itself to be sensed from afar, from the indeterminate, charged with excessive loneliness which has nothing to do with you.

And it only allows itself to be sensed feelingly, through temperature, and through a sorrow that has nothing to do with you.

If anything fills me with awe, it is the image that imagines me from afar;

a breathing heard at my core. The body breathes at my core.

Darkness rivets me—the body's night rivets me.

The body of the night and the death of the body rivet my mind.

❦   ❦   ❦

And I ask myself:

¿Qué es tu cuerpo? Yo no sé si te has preguntado alguna vez qué es tu cuerpo.

Es un trance grave y difícil.

Yo me he acercado una vez a mi cuerpo;

y habiendo comprendido que jamás lo había visto, aunque lo llevaba a cuestas,

le he preguntado quién era;

y una voz, en el silencio, me ha dicho:

Yo soy el cuerpo que te habita, y estoy aquí, en las oscuridades, y te duelo, y te vivo, y te muero.

Pero no soy tu cuerpo. Yo soy la noche.

What is your body? I don't know whether you've even asked yourself.

It's a gambit, grave and adverse.

One time I came close to my body;

and realizing I had never seen it, even though I bore it with me,

I asked it who it was;

and a voice, in the silence, said to me:

I am the body who inhabits you, and I am here in the darkness, and I suffer you, and live you, and die you.

But I am not your body. I am the night.

Afterword

Journey to the Center of *The Night*

> For myself I like to take my sorrow into the
> shadow of the old monasteries, my guilt into
> cloisters and under tapestries, and into the
> misericordes of unimaginable cantinas where sad-
> faced porters and legless beggars drink at dawn,
> whose cold jonquil beauty one rediscovers in death.
> —Malcolm Lowry, *Under the Volcano*

In its latest edition, The Royal Academy's *Dictionary of the Spanish Language* includes a curious Bolivianism, "ófrico," which it defines as "dark" and "somber." Unlike other Bolivianisms included in the *DSL*, "ófrico," a word Jaime Saenz often used, isn't derived from an indigenous language. It may be a Creole word, but it looks suspiciously like a typographical deformation of "órfico," Orphic, which is how my computer automatically "corrects" the spelling. I believe both terms are useful in considering Jaime Saenz and his work. On the one hand, we constantly encounter dark, even terrifying "ófrican" situations in his books, and on the other hand, like Orpheus, Saenz's poetry in particular—and his work in general—refuses to sidestep the descent into Hell. In fact, darkness and dread are constants with Jaime Saenz, characterizing both his work and his person. But it is important to remember that he treated them with a certain detachment, since for him, the true problem was how (paraphrasing the title of one of his books) "to cross that distance."

Typically, Saenz observed rituals—extremely idiosyncratic ones—that in the long run became hallmarks of the local cult that surrounded him during the final decades of his life: from the artisan-like care he took with first editions of his books to the white, wide-brimmed Panamanian sombrero he wore, from his collection of pocket watches to the mythic anecdotes of his bohemian alcoholic past. Invariably, visits to his house were marked by "Saenzian" protocols. As an illustration, let's pay him a visit.

It is late at night. We're in the Miraflores neighborhood of La Paz, in front of the house where Jaime Saenz lives. His "Auntie Esther," with whom he has lived for many years, opens the door and invites us in. She guides us through the entryway to the stairs and takes her leave. On the second floor, Saenz is waiting in what he calls his "Krupp Studios." After initial greetings, he invites us to sit down by the fireplace, around a circular table that dominates the setting. On the inside cover of his novel, *Felipe Delgado*, there is a photo of Saenz seated at this exact table. A floor lamp illuminates the table laterally; this is a Krupp lamp which reminds us of his trip to Germany and gives the room its moniker. In one of the corners stands a watch-maker's table where various instruments of that trade—one of his hobbies—are spread out. On the wall above, we can make out Enrique Arnal's portrait of him which is reproduced on the cover of the posthumous edition of his first novel, *The Papers of Narciso Lima Achá*. On another wall, above the fireplace, we see a smaller painting, and on the door that leads to the next room (his bedroom), we see a few of the dyed skulls he liked to sketch. One of these sketches illustrates the cover of his book *Lives and Deaths*. Nearby, a large rag doll with a porcelain face keeps us company, seated in its little wicker chair. There are various boxes and cartons in the room, still unpacked, remnants of the most recent and never-definitive move.

And there, hanging as usual from the back of a chair, is his "apara-pita's coat." While we take in other objects (a telescope, a rock crystal they say belonged to Goethe), someone produces a bottle of *singani* (grape brandy and fruit juice) which Saenz pours for the occasion. The dice game of *cacho*, which will be the principle activity of the visit, has already been set up and discussed. One initiate points out that each player must choose his or her own "real" name in order to play. Saenz's is *Jurjizada*, a name also used occasionally by Gurdieff. For the novices, Saenz explains that in his house, the traditional *generala dormida* (casting five identical dice in a single throw) is not the sockdolager. One can still attempt, if the round permits, a *frutti* or, better still, a *tutti frutti*. The *frutti* consists of three different plays, or two of the same play (straight, full, poker, or even *generala*), one after another, and for the *tutti frutti*, three of the same dice play—it doesn't matter which—in a row. Someone mentions that Saenz keeps a register of such feats and recalls that, one time, Silvia Mercedes Ávila achieved a decisive tutti frutti. Also, in order to play, everyone must place a bet; not much, but always something.

Beside the watchmaker's table, standing in front of a window, there is a tall and ancient 78 rpm gramophone, one of those worked with a hand crank. Later, during a break in the game, we'll be treated to original recordings of "Nevando está" and other pieces by Adrián Patiño. While we're playing, it's impossible to ignore that Saenz splits his cigarettes in two before he smokes them. When questioned, he explains that this way he smokes less because he sees twice the number of butts. He hasn't touched alcohol for a long time, but he shares in the toasts with a cup of tea which Auntie Esther, unobserved, places on the table. We stand and drink to the game's decisive plays—two *generalas dormidas* tonight—and exclaim together in English, "Oh, yes!" The principle topics of conversation are the game's avatars. Little or nothing is said of literature, although Saenz promises to read some of his new work at another time—perhaps passages from *The Night*, a book-length poem in progress. For all his rituals and spells, Saenz fails to win and, to change his luck, he takes from a drawer a long, fat pencil with a little plastic hand attached to the point. At his next turn, he gathers the dice with this hand; something like "a change of hands" for a change of luck. But this doesn't help much either. And so the night and the game advance. A final round is played and, after a last toast, it's time to depart. Saenz accompanies us to the doorway and, of course, "enchanted," accepts the promise of a future visit.

To speak about himself and his work, Saenz would often quote a phrase attributed to Columbus and chiseled on the plinth of his statue in Paseo del Prado in La Paz: "To live is not necessary; the necessary thing is to sail." In these words we glimpse the adventurer who wasn't content with immediate reality and wanted to find a new world in this world. Yet, Saenz didn't ignore everyday life; in fact, he lived it intensely and celebrated everything down to the smallest details—objects, stories, people, places in La Paz, for example—as I hope our (imagined) visit to his home has made clear. But he did so with a certain overtone. For him, the quotidian had a profound (immanent) aspect that his work set out to disclose. Overall, the crucial thing for Saenz was the search for something concealed and beyond, the impossible encounter.

The Saenzian quest crosses, as he would say, various distances.

One search delves into the linguistic dimension. To that end, perhaps the best example is his first book (*The Scalpel*, 1955). There, the reader notes expanding circles of meaning suggested by key words. Personally, I believe that in *To Cross This Distance* (1973), Saenz comes to master the language he sought; a very peculiar language, by the way, because it serves above all as a means of inquiry. Secondly, there is a search for a sense of the personal—of the "Who am I?" type—carried out through the ongoing dialogue with an alter ego that is omnipresent, especially in his poetry, and that presents itself by means of the pronoun "you." The interesting thing about this dialogue is that "you" can just as easily point to an immanent "I" as to a more removed "Other." Also, the use of "you" always evokes the participation—albeit indirectly—of the reader. Thirdly, there is a definite transcendental search, one which might be understood as a mystical theology that doesn't attempt to access plenitude directly. Instead, it confronts absence, or as Saenz would say in his own poetic idiom, confronts face to face the darkness and shadows that shroud the plenitude. This will become clearer in my comments on *The Night*, but I want to add that often Saenz roots this transcendental search in its immediate material and cultural surround. Here's an example.

One of Saenz's most famous characters is the *aparapita* of La Paz. An aparapita is an indigenous immigrant—more precisely, an Andean Indian or "Aymara"—who lives in poverty in the city and its fringe neighborhoods. Although one can imagine him as an actual homeless man of the large Western cities, an aparapita is not a drifter or a beggar; mostly, he works as a porter in the public markets or in the transportation centers and stockyards. In Saenz's world, the aparapitas also frequent the garbage dumps and spend their nights drinking alcohol in taverns. When he knows his life has run its course, an aparapita works tirelessly to make enough money to drink himself to death. When he finally dies, his few belongings are inherited by his fellow aparapitas and his anonymous body ends up in the morgue. Nevertheless, according to local beliefs, his "spirit" now protects his friends in the tavern. This ritual, known as "sloughing off the body," highlights the way death reconciles an individual with his community. The aparapita's body dies, but his spirit survives. This concept is part of many mystical traditions, but in the aparapita's case, it stresses the (alcoholic) excesses and the possible transcendence, through death, of such excesses. Recalling Columbus's phrase, one could say that if "to live is not necessary" and "the necessary thing is to sail," in the case of the aparapita, who occupies a key place in the symbology of Saenz's negative mysticism, the boat must voyage into dark, tumultuous waters.

In a critical sense, these waters course through the city of La Paz. As in Joyce's Dublin or Fellini's Rome, Saenz's La Paz is a re-creation of the author. It is said that every seeker essentially suffers from "Ulysses syndrome," the need to (re)encounter the place he came from. The Ithaca of Saenz is *his* La Paz. The figure of the aparapita haunting the city's penetralia has long been a part of the search. In one essay ("The Aparapita of La Paz," 1968), the city of La Paz and its aparapitas blur together in a mutual coming-into-being: the city transforms into the aparapita, and the aparapita transforms into La Paz. One must be familiar with La Paz and the "aparapita's coat" to understand. In both cases, the crucial thing is the conjunction of diverse fragments. Impossible as it is to limn Saenz's private La Paz, I will try nonetheless to point out some of its most trenchant traits.

La Paz spans the length of a ravine that descends like a gash from the Altiplano (4000 meters above sea level) to the east, snaking between the foundations of the Andes' western range. The city has grown up along the banks of the Choqueyapu River, which flows from the mountains into the western valleys and plains. In the distance stands Illimani, the massive, three-peaked mountain that resembles a bird about to take flight, and which, they say, protects the city. It is an explicitly chaotic city, for all of Bolivia's historical periods appear together within it, juxtaposed and without transition— from the pre-Columbian era to our times. Moreover, as the seat of the national government, La Paz has been the most intense and frequent backdrop of Bolivia's social and political conflicts, one of which, as we'll see, is addressed in *The Night*. Out of the many locales connected to the historical and political fragments of this urban collage, the places Saenz most frequented—in life and in his work—were in the oldest neighborhoods on the fringe of the city where he spent his bohemian nights drinking in taverns side by side with immigrant aparapitas. In his *Paceñan Images*, Saenz bright-lines other urban fragments that obsessed him (streets, plazas, characters, locales) which comprise his La Paz. Works like *Felipe Delgado*, *The Rooms*, *The Magnet Rock*, "Santiago de Machaca," and "Mr. Balboa" refine the image of the city still further, populating it with fabulous characters and histories.

The Night was Jaime Saenz's last poem. Published in 1984, a year and some months before his death, the sixty-four-page sequence is considered the culmination of his poetry's late phase, initiated by the books *Bruckner* and *The Umbrae*, both published in 1978. With the exception of *The Scalpel* (1955) and *As the Comet Passes* (1982), which gather relatively brief and discrete poems, all of Saenz's books are extended, serial works, organized around a dominant spiritual or philosophical theme—along the lines of *The Bridge* or *The Waste Land*. Each of these long compositions is a prismatic, self-contained world, although, crucially, key continuities in content and style inform the various collections—continuities that extend into his fiction, as well: the theme of alcoholism, for example, so central to *The Night*, is also at the heart of his novelistic masterpiece, *Felipe Delgado*.

The poem is composed of four movements: "The Night" (I), "The Gatekeeper" (II), "Interval" (III), and, again, "The Night" (IV). Broadly, we could say that the first section introduces the theme by showing alcohol as a paradoxical path of terror and knowledge; "The Gatekeeper" offers a portrait of one of the condemned who has elected this path so he might enter and inhabit the Night (understood of course, throughout the poem, as both literal and figural); "Interval," in a manner reminiscent of *The Inferno*, or a painting by Bosch, details the incidents of "The Massacre of All Saints," a social and political nightmare that befell Bolivia in 1979; and the fourth part, one of the most profoundly mystical passages of twentieth-century Latin American poetry—at once beautiful and disturbing—shows The Night bonded to the body of the initiate who inhabits it.

In a certain sense, the poem is circular, traveling from night to night. Along the way, Saenz mines with manifold meanings the contents of that circle, doing so largely through his favorite rhetorical figures: metonymy in general, and synecdoche in particular. In his hands, relations of proximity are almost always relations of identity, where aspects become wholes and vice versa. In the poem's circle, the two nights are different yet the same, separate yet interfaced with the other. . . . There is, one could say, no escaping the circle.

What is the night for Saenz? I won't try to interpret the entire poem, but I can point out a few trails the text beckons us to follow.

It is important to note that Saenz does not ignore the night's obvious connotations. It is dark and contrasts with the day. But the text emphasizes that "the night" is not so much a time interval as a location, a single space, one that can manifest itself, in shards, during the day. If night is a space, one can be in the night and not only during the night. Saenz also takes up the poetic tradition of relating the night with death, in the legacy of, for example, Dylan Thomas's "Rage, rage against the dying of the light." I won't insult the reader by summing up these indices into some kind of equation that might unlock the mysteries of the work. These are only very basic starting points, and Saenz offers the reader an entire world of possibilities.

Although it is linked with death, the night is not an antagonistic space—as with death, it is uncomfortable and even terrible, but never antagonistic. To know the night implies a knowledge—"sageness," the ancients would say—of life, death, and the sensual world. Of course, this knowledge is not easy, and accessing it is difficult, as the alcoholic finds. Saenz had his own term to indicate the magnitude of that knowledge. What he calls "jubilation" characterizes most of his work. But "jubilation" is complex, a mingling of ecstasy, enigma, and terror, like the mood conjured up by Ahab in his mad pursuit of Moby Dick. The reader will encounter this term and its reverberations throughout *The Night.*

Although meant to be mystical in spirit, *The Night* is also meant to be circumstantial, even topical. In that regard, the most vivid images and scenes are those of the third part ("Interval"). Making explicit reference to "November," they are clearly related to the "Massacre of All Saints" when, in 1979, on November 1–2, the date for the festival celebration of All Saints, a short-lived coup spearheaded by General Natush Busch interrupted the democratic process and crushed popular resistance in a massacre. The images of Saenz's "Interval" connote the horror of social repression. On the one hand, this part can be read as an act of poetic protest; on the other, the terror indicated by its verses is also indicative of the night's contents— its dark jubilation.

The historical impulse also informs the "Gatekeeper" section of the poem, as the speaker's voice recalls a series of objects he has left behind over the course of his life. This enumeration is typical of Saenz, biographically as well as stylistically: many of these objects played a part in his own life. The relational symbol of "Auntie Esther" is one of the more obvious examples of the way Saenz built into his work a ghostly memorial record, a wraith-like narrative with touches of wit and irony.

Indeed, because of its themes, Saenz's poetry is typically read as metaphysical and solemn. But even in its heaviest moments, it behooves the reader to pay attention to the distances his poetry often creates through ironic humor. In his poetry, this distancing is necessary to keep from getting lost in the fascination of the (terrible) jubilation that he pursues. For example, in the enumeration of objects mentioned above, after evoking familiar pieces of furniture, Saenz reflects: "What's it all worth, I ask myself." He answers: "Well, in truth, not much, and even under best circumstances, not enough to buy a ranga-ranga." The "ranga-ranga" is a popular soup whose principle ingredient is precisely a "ranga" cut into little chunks.

Could it be a coincidence that the "ranga" or cow's intestine is also called the "book" or "booklet" of a cow? Nostalgia, distance, irony, popular traditions, and, possibly, also literature (book/booklet) almost imperceptibly interchange their meanings in that ironic meditation that is determined by and in death.

The principal character of the poem's final part is the body. In pointing out Saenz's various ontological quests and noting the interlocutory "you," I didn't mention the more immediate presence, the one that accompanies us even in the most radical solitude: our body itself. I don't wish to detail through any single illustration the complex relationships that Saenz establishes between the body, the "I/you," and the other elements of the poem. However, I believe that a broad formal unity can be suggested. Saenz's poems do not necessarily "tell a story," but they do always assume a latent plot that shows itself as a kind of *ouroboros* by the end. In their different ways, the poems of Saenz presuppose a type of poetic suspense that circles back into resolution. In *The Night*, the body will be the protagonist of this final articulation. As it will be for us all.

Luis H. Antezana
Cochabamba, October, 2003